Create Your Own

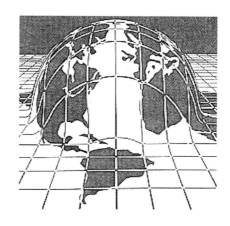

Mark Neely & Sarina Kreitmeier

NET.WORKS

NET.WORKS

**Net.Works, PO Box 200
Harrogate, N.Yorks
HG1 2YR   England**

**http://www.net-works.co.uk
Email: sales@net-works.co.uk
UK Fax: 01423-526035**

Net.Works is an imprint of Take That Ltd.

Published in association with Maximedia Pty Ltd
PO Box 529 Kiama, NSW 2533, Australia.

ISBN: 1 873668 42 2
© 1998 Take That Ltd. & Maximedia Pty Ltd

10 9 8 7 6 5 4 3 2 1

Trademarks:
Trademarked names are used throughout this book. Rather than place a trademark symbol in every occurance of a trademark name, the names are being used only in an editorial fashion for the benefit of the trademark owner, with no intention to infringe the trademark.

Printed and bound in The United Kingdom

Disclaimer:
The information in this book is distributed on an "as is" basis, without warranty. While very effort has been made to ensure that this book is free from errors or omissions, neither the author, the publisher, or their respective employees and agents, shall have any liability to any person or entity with respect to any liability, loss or damage caused or alleged to have been caused directly or indirectly by advice or instructions contained in this book or by the computer hardware or software products described herein. **Readers are urged to seek prior expert advice before making decisions, or refraining from making decisions, based on information or advice contained in this book.**

Throughout this book you will find web addresses on various subjects. These will help you get started with your web site. However, just like 'real life' addresses, some may have changed since going to press. We hope this does not spoil your enjoyment.

Contents

Change of Address

When you try to access some of the sites recommended in this book you may come across the dreaded "file not found" screen or a similar message indicating the site is no longer located at the given address.

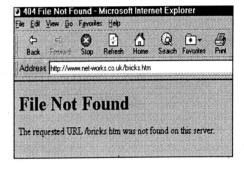

This isn't because we have given you the wrong address or mis-typed it (though that may have happened, because we are only human!) but because the World Wide Web is in a constant stage of flux.

Every day pages are being created, but also others disappear. Perhaps a company or person has a page on a certain ISP's computer, but they found a cheaper way to access the World Wide Web and changed ISP. So they have to take their page with them and load it onto another computer.

However there are a few tricks that you can try to locate the information you are after (assuming you have already checked that you've typed the address exactly as given):

❑   Try changing the file name extension from ***.htm** to ***.html** and visa versa.

❑   Add or subtract the **www** at the beginning of the page address.

❑   Play around with the **capitalisation** of the address, but remember that host names are not case sensitive.

❑   Remove the last part of the file name so that you are just left with the **host name**. You can then follow links on the site to try and find the page that you require.

If all else fails take a few key words from the page you are trying to find and go to a search engine. Even if this still does not find the site that you require you will at least find similar sites and perhaps still get the information you are after.

Chapter 1

Why the Web?

Imagine for a moment that you own a clothes store in a busy shopping high street. In the last few years, your shop — like most in the retail industry — has endured flat consumer spending and pressures on profit margins. Although you've established market share, your cash flow is often barely enough to cover running expenses such as operating, rent, staffing and advertising. In short, times are tough.

Now imagine further that a complete stranger walks in off the street and says that you can halve your advertising costs, reduce your rental by over two-thirds, slash operating stock expenses and never pay staff costs again. You'd think you were being taken for a ride.

But this is exactly what many people say the World Wide Web can do — and it has plenty of business people very excited!

On the other hand, you may have spent years researching your family tree. You've put the data together and can create an exciting historical story based around your extended family. It would be a shame to keep all your research to yourself. So you could create a 'personal' web page and publish your findings on the Web. Now everyone with the same surname may be able benefit from your efforts and might even be able to contribute some further details.

Your personal web page need not stop there. You may wish to put up details of meetings for your local sports or social club. You could write a book of your own and see it published around the world (on the web), or you could even create a page with pictures of you and your pets (don't laugh, thousands have done it!).

Whatever your aims, if you want people to see your information, easily and cheaply, the World Wide Web is the place to put it.

Automated sales medium

The Web has many uses, and we will examine some of the more impressive later in this chapter. But the most widely perceived use for the Web is as an automated sales medium. The basic concept is fairly simple, borrowing as it does from the mail-order business model popularised in the late 80s and early 90s. In essence, a vendor establishes a Web site that contains an online catalogue of its products. In the example of the clothes shop, such a catalogue would contain colour photos of each item of clothing (perhaps multiple photos to demonstrate different colours or sizes), together with a text description of the item (such as design issues, material quality or washing options). Consumers would visit the site, view the catalogue and place orders for items using their credit card, which would be shipped to them directly.

The advantages of online catalogues are many:

✔ The vendor can display items and accept orders 24 hours a day, seven days a week.

✔ Customers on the other side of the globe find it as easy as local customers to examine and order from the online catalogue.

✔ The sales process – display, order placement and processing – is automated, which can reduce staff and associated overheads.

✔ There are no costly long-term leases and associated overheads: hiring space on a Web server is very inexpensive.

✔ The payment process can be automated, with funds automatically credited to your bank account.

✔ Paperwork – such as order forms, invoices etc. – can be minimised or even completely avoided.

✔ Inventories can be stocked on a 'just-in-time" basis, freeing up important capital.

Many businesses have incorporated the Web into their sales strategy – ranging from retail giants such as Tesco (www.tesco.co.uk) and Sainsbury's (www.sainsburys.co.uk) to smaller business (like our own www.net-works.co.uk site) and home-based companies. But the Web offers businesses more benefits than simply online sales.

The Web is the perfect selling platform for niche, hard to find consumer goods, such as books, CDs, gifts etc. The World of Gambling established its Web site (www.gamble.co.uk) to cater to this market, combining an extensive range of goodies with a simple, online shopping process.

If you're looking for anything to do with horse racing, football betting, casinos, or any form of wagering, you will probably find it here.

Customer service functions

Many businesses find their Web site(s) to be extremely profitable - and not only in terms of sales. Web sites are ideally suited to customer loyalty initiatives, helping businesses generate additional revenues from repeat sales while reducing operating overheads by automating customer service functions.

Perhaps the best example of this sort of customer service is provided by the banking industry.

It wasn't that long ago that "doing the banking" meant a tedious routine of filling out a mountain of paperwork, driving to the (often not so) local branch, and then queuing for a clerk. Today bank customers can make payments, arrange funds transfers, query account issues, and obtain balances and details of recent transactions — all without leaving their desk or filling out a single form.

The most impressive aspect of this type of online customer service is that all parties benefit. Customers save time and reduce their paperwork burden by accessing their account details and performing their banking online. With the right software, customers can even "synchronise" their individual or company accounts and bank balances. For instance, rather than have a bookkeeper manually reconcile business accounts, many businesses can now instruct their accounting software to query their bank's database and transaction records automatically to verify the week's banking — a few hours' work accomplished in a matter of seconds.

Banks benefit too. As consumers migrate to online banking services, banks can reduce spending on staffing, consolidate their network of branches and reduce floor space requirements. This in turn leads to more efficient service delivery, which is often reflected in both reduced bank fees and enhanced profits (good if you are a shareholder!).

Technical support functions

Most retail, industrial and professional sectors are under increasing pressure to make their products and services stand out from the rest of the pack, in an effort to maintain or increase market share. One of the strategies that many companies are employing to achieve this is offering better after-sales support.

Say your new Toyota's engine started making a funny noise, which you think might be related to a loose fan belt. You could either take it to the nearest Toyota service centre (which might be inconvenient, as you will be without your car for part of the day), or you could have a go at resolving the problem yourself. This could be a simple task — if you're familiar with cars. But what if you're not? You could read the owner's guide to see if that gave any pointers, or you could go out and buy a "fix-it" guide. Alternatively you could call Toyota's maintenance help line (if they have one).

A faster, cheaper and potentially less stressful option would be to visit Toyota's Web site (owner.toyota.com) and read the information available on car maintenance.

Toyota's online vehicle maintenance site serves a number of purposes. First of all, it provides Toyota vehicle owners with a valuable service: they can seek information about their car whenever they need it, regardless of the time or day. Second, from Toyota's perspective, it is a cost-effective means of providing extra value to clients, so as to make their vehicles more attractive. More importantly, it allows them to reduce customer-support overheads. For every owner who finds the solution to his or her problem via the Toyota Web site, there is one fewer call to Toyota looking for assistance — and lower staff and telephone costs.

Marketing

Each year, businesses spend billions of pounds marketing their products and services to consumers. We see commercials on TV, videos, billboards and the sides of cars and buses, in newspapers, magazines and in the cinema. We hear commercials on the radio, whilst on hold on the telephone, and as we walk around shopping centres. Some of this marketing is pretty much hit and miss (such as TV and radio advertising); other marketing campaigns are more focused (such as direct mail catalogues).

The Web offers businesses a new marketing medium. Web marketing lets vendors target their audiences very specifically, either by setting up their own sites or by buying advertising space on other sites (to raise brand awareness or to lure customers to their shop or Web site).

If a pharmacy established a Web site, for instance, it could be quite confident that each visitor constitutes a "pre-qualified" consumer. In other words, with hundreds of thousands of other possible Web destinations, it is very unlikely that consumers would visit the pharmacy's Web site unless they were actually interested in the products or services on offer.

Many of the Web sites used in the media as examples of successful online retail and wholesale businesses are US-based. But Europeans have not been slouchers when it comes to leveraging the Internet to enhance profits.

With this knowledge, the site owner can tailor its content and sales focus purely on the needs of the consumer, without having to invest time and effort developing content that seeks to stimulate the visitor's interest in its products or services. Put simply, if the consumer is there to buy or learn about the vendor's products, then the vendor can get straight to the selling and educating process.

At the other end of the marketing spectrum, a golf club vendor might place banner ads promoting its products on a general sport Web site, or one specifically related to golf (like the PGA's Web site, www.pga.com). In both instances it can be fairly confident that visitors to the various Web sites displaying its advertisements are *more likely* (although there is no guarantee) to be interested in its products, as they have pre-qualified themselves by visiting golf or sports-related Web sites.

It is this level of targeting that most excites online vendors and advertisers. It is quite difficult to achieve these levels of targeting with television and other forms of broadcast advertising. While it may be possible with special interest programs and print publications, their format does not offer the flexibility inherent in online advertising, and few can offer the breadth of audience that online advertising commands.

Interactivity

The ability to interact with consumers has long been the Holy Grail of the marketing profession. Even the best crafted print advert or the most visually appealing television advertising can only do so much for the marketing of a product or service.

For example, a travel agency might take out a full-page newspaper advertisement advising readers of its Christmas discounted flights. Because of the expense

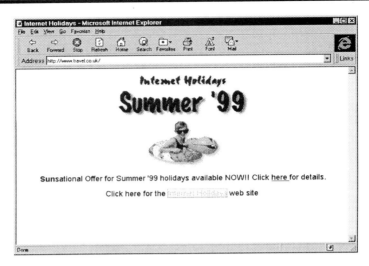

The market for online travel bookings is enormous, and growing rapidly.

involved in such advertising, the travel agency can only promote a selection of its discounted flights. This can severely limit the effectiveness of the advertisement. First of all, not every reader will be interested in travel information or discounted flights. Of those that are, not all will be interested in the specific travel options mentioned in the advertisement.

Therefore, the advertisement has at least a two-fold objective: to let those readers who are interested in specific travel products know what the agency is offering, and to convince those interested in travel products other than those mentioned in the advertisement to pick up the phone or drop into one of its outlets. The advertisement must inspire an impulsive reaction — convincing the reader then and there that they should make contact with the advertiser. If this is not achieved, then the travel agent has not maximised the benefit of its advertising.

The interactive nature of the Web means that online advertising does not suffer from these limitations or problems. For instance, there is no reason why a travel agency's Web site could not list all of its travel and associated products. But more importantly, rather than bombard each visitor to its Web site with a host of travel packages, the Web site could be used to actively market according to each individual customer's requirements.

A typical travel agency Web site experience might go something like this: A consumer is researching her holiday options for the Christmas period. She has already decided that she would like to travel abroad, but is undecided where. She connects to the travel agency's Web site and is offered a few generic travel options, including cruises, tropical resort flight/hotel packages and ski holiday packages.

Liking the idea of spending Christmas in the snow, she clicks on that link and is taken to the section of the Web site marketing ski holidays. After reviewing the available packages, she does not find one that suits her particular interests. If she's going to go skiing, she'd like to visit Aspen, Hollywood's favourite ski destination. There's not a specific package listed. However, as this is a net-savvy travel agency, they have created a "do-it-yourself" holiday planning utility.

By answering a few specific questions (including preferred airline, accommodation preferences and the like), the agency's Web site is able to scan its database of flights and other travel options and put together a tailored holiday package for the consumer. Delighted with the service and excited by the thought of spending Christmas in the snow, she books the trip and pays online with her credit card.

Had the agency not been able to offer individualised service, it is likely that it would have lost a profitable sale. No other advertising medium allows the vendor to get this "close" to consumers, and respond directly to their specific needs.

Other motivations

Of course, the Web is not constituted solely of for-profit sites. There are quite a number of Web sites whose aim it is to educate or otherwise inform Internet users. For example, there are many hobbyist Web sites, containing information about the favourite hobbies of their owners and the organisations that they belong to. There are public service Web sites, such as those operated by the World Wildlife Fund (www.wwf.org) and Planet Ark (www.planetark.org). And, finally, there are general announcement services and resources, such as online newspapers, encyclopaedias, search engines, tutorials and how-to's.

The benefits of an Internet presence are not limited to big business.

While these sites might not be planned around the concept of interacting with and selling to customers etc., they should still adhere to the basic design and communication principles espoused in this book.

Conclusion

In the following chapter, we will examine the fundamental steps involved in designing, creating and implementing a Web site. For the main part, the focus will be on creating business Web sites, as this is likely to be what the majority of readers of this book are interested in. However, we will also examine some of the issues peculiar to other, non-commercial Web sites.

Further Reading

There is probably more "Web print" devoted to the business potential of the Internet than any other topic. Here is a short list of excellent resources for those who want to learn more about using the Internet for business:

InternetWorld - www.internetworld.com

NetProfit Magazine - www.netprofit-mag.com

Net-Profit Centre - www.net-profit-center.net

Doing Business Online - www.canbus.com/dbo/cbnews.htm

EMarketer - www.e-land.com

Communications Week Interactive – techweb.cmp.com/ia/iad_web_/

Web Commerce Today - www.wilsonweb.com/wct/

Internet.com's Electronic Commerce Guide - e-comm.internet.com

Two books are available from Net.Works:
The Complete Beginner's Guide to Making Money on the Internet by ALex Kiam at £3.95, and
The Expert's Business Guide to the Internet By Mark Neely at £24.95

Chapter 2

Planning Your Web Site

When it comes to creating Web sites, one of the first - and most important - questions that you should ask yourself is: "Why do I want a Web site"? Jumping straight in without a specific goal or a defined purpose usually leads to wasted time and a Web site that is at best ineffective, and which could potentially even hurt your business.

Your primary considerations will be along the lines of:

✔ What am I trying to achieve with my Web site?
✔ Who do I wish to attract to it?
✔ What will the Web site offer to attract these people?
✔ What benefits will it offer?

Other considerations may include:

✔ Is the Web site intended to make a profit, be revenue neutral or contribute to the business in other ways (such as reduce communication costs and service overseas markets, etc.)?
✔ How much time and effort am I prepared to put into maintaining and updating the Web site?
✔ Will the Web site be constituted primarily of links to other sites, or will it feature original content?

Once you have examined the reasons for your Web site, and the purposes that it will fulfil, you will be in a better position to plan and create it.

Plan, plan and then plan some more

Most large corporate Web sites benefit from a team of professionals such as graphic designers, marketers and copywriters. Even if your resources are limited, you can still learn many lessons from industry behemoths like Toyota (www.toyota.com), IBM (www.ibm.com) and Sony (www.sony.com). One thing you can learn is the importance of the planning process.

It is important when planning your Web site that you have everything at hand so there is no time-wasting. You should have an outline of the various pieces of information that your Web site will contain (preferably already divided into logical segments), a list of images or graphics that you plan to use (if not the actual images themselves) and a list of related Web sites if you plan offering visitors directions to other sites of interest. You should also work to a written plan, to avoid duplication and omissions. Here's a checklist that you can adapt to your specific needs:

❑ Decide who your target audience will be. Whom are you trying to reach? What is important to them? How can you meet their needs?

❑ Research existing Web sites. You should look at what your competitors offer on their sites, as well as examine other sites of interest to see if they generate any ideas for yours.

❑ Gather the content — in other words, the "guts" of your Web site, what visitors actually read and see.

❑ Figure out what resources you will need, such as graphics, online ordering forms and feedback areas.

❑ Decide on the size of your site. How big do you expect your site to be? How much information do you want to offer, and how many pages (that is, screens of text) does this equate to?

❑ Prepare a flowchart of your site, indicating which pages link to where and the major "pathways" your visitors will be following.

❑ Devise a timeline. How long will the design and creation process take? When do you plan to "launch" your Web site? How often will it need updating?

❑ Assess the costs involved in publishing a Web site, including Web hosting charges, time spent updating and maintaining the Web site, and any charges incurred in hiring third parties to perform tasks beyond your skills (such as specialised graphics and programming).

❑ Give consideration to the security requirements of your Web site, or any other special programming required. If you plan to accept credit card details online for payment purchases, you will almost certainly want to offer secure transaction facilities. If your Web site is quite large, or is to be frequently updated, you might consider offering a search feature, so that visitors can quickly locate the information that they want.

It is important to realise the distinction between pages of information and screens of information. In general, there are no hard and fast rules governing the relationship between the amount of words in a given Web page, and how many screens it requires to display it.

Identifying your target audience

Publishing Web sites is no longer a case of "Build it and they will come". There are now hundreds of thousands of Web sites, all competing for users' attention. Your goal should be to differentiate your Web site – to make it stand out from the crowd. Devising a strategy for achieving this is the most challenging aspect of creating your Web site.

If you offer the most compelling content and satisfy visitors' needs, you enhance the prospect of securing an eventual sale. Before you can do this, of course, you must identify your target audience. Here is a set of questions to help you determine the nature of your target audience:

- Geographic — does your Web site target individuals from a specific country, region, or city, or is it of global reach? Are you likely to attract only English-speaking visitors, or will your site be multi-lingual?

- Demographic — what age group are you trying to attract? Is your potential visitor male or female, or either?

- Psychographic — what stages of life are your visitors in? Are they young optimists who are still studying? Are they married with children? Are they professional working people.

- Behavioural — what sort of personality are you aiming for (for example, reserved or outgoing) and what are their hobbies or interests? What are they consuming?

Design for your audience

Having defined your target audience, your next step is to ensure that the overall design, layout and content of your Web site are both attractive and stimulating to that audience.

If you were looking to attract adolescents to your Web site, for instance, you might want to draw heavily on popular techno-culture to create the impression that the site has some 'street cred' and that it understands them. The cooler your site, the more likely those visitors will tell their friends (word-of-mouth advertising is the best way of attracting interested users to your Web site).

A good example of this type of presentation is DIY Search (www.diysearch.com). Its owners have created an effective - and cool - site using a subtle contrast approach to graphics and colours (OK, it's mainly black and white).

DIY Search is essentially a Search Engine/Web directory of "cool" places to visit. Most of the pages use black text on a white background, with vertical black columns containing white text. Although limited, the overall appearance is quite interesting and eye catching.

With all the multimedia wizardry available on some sites, DIYSearch's simple but stylish approach is quite refreshing.

Web sites aimed at an even younger audience, say, children browsing with their parents, will need a completely different look. They should be "soft and cuddly" enough for the children – with bright colours, simple navigation options, plenty of interesting icons and other forms of visual stimulation – while maintaining a "respectable" appearance to convince their parents that it is an appropriate place for children to explore. Examples of this kind of design can be found at Disney's Daily Blast Web site (www.disney.com/Kids) and SeussVille (www.randomhouse.com/seussville/)

Children will appreciate the bright colours and appealing characters.

If your Web site is aimed at business types, then you will obviously need a completely different approach. Many corporate Web sites adopt conservative yet appealing colours, projecting an image of respectability and dependability. Text layout and images tend to mimic the designs used in business magazines - heavy use of blue and green (colours often associated with tradition and respectability) and subtle graphics and images that neither overpower the reader nor detract from the text.

A good example of this type of design is The Financial Times (www.ft.com). It makes strong use of the traditional newspaper 'pink', with a nice sans-serif font, giving a crisp, efficient look.

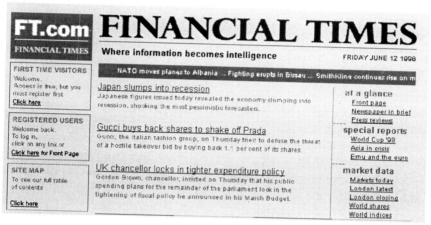

Explore other Web sites

If you are uncertain what type of design you should use on your Web site, spend a few hours (or even a few days if you have the time) wandering around the Web, taking notes of what catches your eye and what you do and don't like. Pick out the central themes (such as colour usage and image presentation), and decide for yourself what "works".

Pay particular attention to issues such as why you linger at a particular site or why you want to abandon it. Do the navigational tools (such as buttons and links) encourage you to explore the Web site, or do they hinder your progress through the site? (Chapter 3 discusses how to use navigational tools in your own site.) Is the site easy to read, or cluttered and too brightly coloured? Does it load quickly, or are you cooling your heels for minutes at a time (a long time by Web-surfing standards)?

It is a good idea to take in some Web sites whose role is similar to that of your planned site. For instance, if you are looking to create a Web site to sell gift baskets featuring your homemade jam to higher-income online shoppers, examine sites offering similar gift items to an upmarket audience.

Be careful, though, that you are not just picking the best qualities from other Web site for your own site. While this will probably save you time in the design process, it might result in something of a loss of identity in terms of your own Web site and what it is trying to say. More importantly, it could result in a Web site that looks poorly planned: a site that is merely a hotchpotch of good ideas is still a hotchpotch!

Gather your content

Ok. So you now understand what you want your Web site to say, whom it is saying it to, and how it will look to its audience. Now it is just a simple matter of writing what it is you want to say, right?

Wrong.

Before you actually start writing your content, do a little brainstorming. Write down an exhaustive list of possible topics and points of interest. Then ask a friend or colleague to read over your ideas and provide feedback on which of your points are solid, interesting ideas and which are really on the fringe in terms of interest or relevance. It would be particularly helpful if this person is someone who might be within your target audience.

Don't get too attached to your list of points, and be prepared to act on the feedback that you receive, eliminating points that are unnecessary or uninteresting. Once you have finalised your outline of what it is that you want say with your Web site, make sure that it fits within your original plan for the Web site. It may be that you need to review either your overall purpose in light of the ideas you came up with, or vice versa.

Conclusion

The lesson that you should have learnt from this chapter is that, in order to develop a meaningful, interesting and focused Web site, you need to plan every aspect of it thoroughly, before you spend your first penny or write your first word of content. Creating a Web site is more than simply throwing text and graphics together on a page. It is all about creating communication.

Once you have planned your Web site, designing it should be a matter of "joining the dots" (well, okay, maybe it won't be that easy!). We take a look at the design process in the next chapter.

Chapter 3

Designing Your Web Site

If your Web site is fun, intelligent, creative and clearly designed, it will go a long way towards helping you stand out from the crowd. Whilst there might be many Web sites offering the same information or services as your planned Web site, few will score highly in terms of both interesting content and appealing presentation. Many Web sites tend to be amateurish affairs, offering either interesting content or appealing presentation, but rarely both.

Once you have completed the planning process, you should be ready to start work on your Web site. Even if you plan to hire a Web design consultant to do the actual "leg work" in creating your Web site, it is still quite important that you have a clear understanding of how the finished product will look. After all, consultants do not work for free and they will no doubt be very happy to listen to you talk your way around deciding what you actually want.

If you have the design aspects of your site worked out to your own satisfaction (even if you do not get into the fine details of each page), you will be able to better brief your consultant, and save yourself time and money in the overall process.

An effective design will present information in a clear, easy-to-read format, and make navigation straightforward and intuitive. Any time a visitor has to stop and puzzle over what you mean or where they can go next, you run the risk of losing them completely as they give up and go look at someone else's site.

Your goal is not to win awards for creativity. It is to service customers, make sales etc. The guiding principle, then, should be: **Design for communication, Not for design's sake.**

Writing style

Writing for the Web isn't quite the same as preparing a report or other business documentation. Sure, your visitors want to read accurate, hype-free information, but they don't want to feel like they are wading through an annual report or internal memo. By all means research your content, and make it as accurate and as reliable as possible. Pay close attention to grammar and spelling, as mistakes will reflect badly on you. However, you need to remember that you are trying to communicate with an audience from a wide variety of backgrounds and levels of technical sophistication. Your writing style should be breezy, even conversational. Avoid unnecessary jargon or trade references.

High-quality, interesting content is the most important aspect of your Web site. Everything else is secondary. Users will forgive a clumsy navigational system if you offer second-to-none content, but they won't forgive poor content, no matter how well it is presented.

Try to recall your first attempt to read your school chemistry or biology textbook. There can be no doubting that these books are authoritative sources of information. But for the majority of readers, they are almost impenetrable. All the necessary information is there, but their presentation and writing style can bore even the most inquisitive of minds within the first couple of paragraphs.

There are quite a number of Web sites like this. Their creators got carried away with being authoritative and exhaustive, and forgot that the basic aim of the Web site was to communicate with readers. Whereas school science students are (usually) motivated to try and make sense of their textbooks, Web users are not so forgiving.

Page layout and visual design

Research has shown that Web users, as a rule, have short attention spans. This is not because of some sort of communal attention deficit disorder; rather it is the result of the fact that most users pay for the time they spend online (and as such their online time is limited) and that there are a large number of interesting sites to visit. Additionally, some of the popular Web sites have raised the level standards-wise, and visitors are quick to scorn an amateurish site.

You should ensure that you have eye-catching graphics or headlines that will immediately inform visitors of what is on offer at your Web site. If visitors have to browse through two or more screens to get a hint about the purpose of your Web site, they will leave.

Try to keep each page small enough to fit entirely within the user's screen. Many users will not scroll down to read information or to look for options that are beyond what they can see right away. If you must have Web pages that are, individually, longer than a single screen, ensure that all the important headlines and links are within the first screen.

Be careful not to overcrowd your page. Simplicity with a little imagination is always more effective than a page where the reader does not know where to begin reading. Maintain a sensible balance between content and illustrations. Break up long sections of text with subheadings, bulleted lists, and graphics: a screen full of text is very tiring to read — much more so than a paper page full of type.

Unless the topic of your Web site dictates either an all-text or all-graphic Web site, maintain a sensible balance between the two. Items like graphic icons and horizontal dividers can be used both as a text presentation tool and as a means of dividing sections of text into logical or "bite-sized" portions.

Make use of graphics or clip art to demonstrate your points or to highlight sections of information so users know where to look for what interests them. (Chapters 4 and 5 discuss Web graphics in detail.)

Avoid clashes between your foreground and background colours. While newsprint, for example, traditionally features black ink on a white background, the Web allows a mixture of foreground and background colours. Feel free to experiment in order to find a colour to suit your site's proposed image, but always ensure that there is sufficient contrast between your selection of background and foreground colours so that users need not strain to read your content.

Avoid using frames. They rob Internet users of some of the most important Web browsing tools — for instance, the ability to bookmark a specific page so that they can return directly to it in future without having to weave through a Web site. Also, extensive use of frames may make it difficult for visitors to print the various pages of your Web site.

The layout of your Web site is very much a subjective matter, but it is important that you do in fact have a general template, and maintain it throughout the site. While applying several different layout styles to your Web site might make it artistically impressive, it will only serve to confuse visitors, as the absence of a clear and dominant layout will rob your Web site of intuitive navigation cues.

Navigation

One of the most crucial, but often underrated, aspects of your Web site is its navigational elements. Unless you are planning only a single-page Web site, you will need to provide visitors with the means of finding their way around.

Browsing through a Web site differs from browsing, say, a book: there are no "tops" and "bottoms" of pages, no way to "feel" how far you've progressed through it by compar-

'Frames' is a feature supported by most Web browsers that allows the area displayed on-screen by a Web browser to be divided into two or more sections (frames). Frames can be very convenient, as they allow the use of different styles and navigational elements within a single screen, but they should generally be avoided because not all browsers support them. Those which do tend to interpret frames in different ways, which can lead to difficulties in controlling how your Web site is displayed on the visitor's screen.

ing how many pages are in each hand. It's easy for visitors to get disoriented on a badly structured site. Worse, they may very well decide that trying to blunder their way around such a site is not worth the trouble.

Most Web sites revolve around their "home page". The home page is the first or opening page of a Web site, where visitors begin their explorations. Your home page acts as an introduction and gateway to the contents of your site, just as a magazine's cover introduces readers to its content. Home pages generally lead with a catchy headline, banner or logo and a short introduction to the site. This is generally followed by a series of clickable hyperlinks (Chapter 6 discusses these in detail) that will take visitors to the different sections of the site.

Traditionally, we tend to view information as a linear resource — start at the beginning and read to the end. The Web is transforming the way that that we use and absorb information. Readers are no longer bound to read information in the order in which it is presented. This makes it imperative that you consider as an integral part of your site's design the navigation "pathways" you will provide to your visitors. The simplest form of navigation is to include a text-based overview of your Web site — such as a one- or two-paragraph description — on the home page, with links to the site's various areas. Visitors read the description and click on the appropriate hyperlink to move to the area they want. This type of navigation is simple and effective.

If your Web site contains many different areas and corresponding pages of text, visitors might be turned off by the thought of having to read through a lengthy site description looking for areas of interest. In such cases you might design your home page to act more like a table of contents, providing a skeletal overview of — and links to — the major areas of your Web site. Each linked area could in turn contain easily digestible summaries that visitors could use to jump straight to the resource of interest.

To make their sites more appealing and intuitive, many designers use icons to represent different areas. Common examples are question mark icons ("?") to represent a link to the help (or "frequently asked questions") section, and pound signs ("£") or credit card symbols to represent a link to the online ordering section.

However, the nature of your Web site might be such that you can not easily use icons to represent its various areas, or it might be of such a size that you couldn't really fit the icons necessary for site navigation on a single Web page. In this case, you need to devise a logical structure for your Web site — which is often an art form in itself!

If your Web site consists of more than a handful of pages, try to divide its content areas into logical sections, with a summary of each section on your home page. Assume, for example, that you were developing an online bookstore. What is the best way to categorise your offerings so that you can work out a neat, easy-to-follow navigational structure? You might decide to go for absolute simplicity, and offer only two options on the first page: Fiction and Non-Fiction. Depending on the size of your offerings, this might be a workable solution, and you could offer further categories on the corresponding pages.

But let's say that your offerings are quite substantive, so you will need a few more links from the main page to make the Web site more manageable. Your visits to a few online bookstores have shown that the average online bookstore has no more than five category options on its opening page, so you decide to go with this (research has indicated that five options or choices are the maximum that the average person can easily work with).

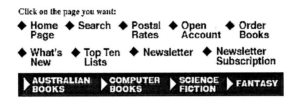

Users may find the number of options available on the homepage of the Bookworm Web site overwhelming.

You break your book categories into Reference, Sport, Sci-Fi, True Crime and Best Sellers. You plan to rely heavily on "guest" book reviews (supplied by customers), so you include a link to your Book Review section, taking your number of links on the first page to six. Obviously an online bookstore needs to be a little more specific with its categorisation, so you decide to offer subcategory pages, with no more than four subcategories on each.

To help you in the planning of your web site, you may find it useful to draw a flowchart, showing exactly where each page links to and from. This will help you both in terms of preparing content (you'll know which bit goes where), but also in arranging hyperlinks from page to page. It will also help you analyse whether your proposed "signposts", such as icons, will make sense to visitors (be sure to ask friends and colleagues for their feedback).

Avoid overly complex Web sites. As a general rule of thumb, users should not have to click more than three (yes, three) links within your site to get the information that they are looking for. Don't bury your content deep inside your site. Remember that visitors may have a short attention span, so if getting to the content that interests them takes too much effort, they won't stick around!

One final point should be made in terms of designing the flow of your Web site: there should be no "dead ends". Your Web site should never have "orphan" pages — pages that are not integrated into the site. In other words, you need to ensure that each individual page of your Web site gives visitors a way to go somewhere else. Every single page of your Web site should contain navigational items, even if they are simply "back to home page" or "return to previous page" links.

Consistency

The most important 'tool' that you have to make your site effective is consistency. Consistency reassures your visitors that you have taken the trouble to consider their needs, and makes their visit to your site more pleasant for them and more productive for you.

If you are predictable in your use of subheading styles and graphics, your visitors will be able to keep a mental picture of how you've structured your information. For example, if you use a particular size font for the title of a new topic, always use the same size font each time you introduce a new topic. If you once use a smaller version of your logo as an icon that visitors can click on to go back to the home page, use the same icon on all pages to mean "go back to the home page" — and have that be the only thing you use it for. If you use a series of icons arranged in a row to give visitors a choice of places to go, make that arrangement absolutely consistent from page to page. If you want to put information at the bottom of each page (such as your email address and other contact information), make sure you format it the same way each time it appears.

Avoiding common pitfalls

Many Webmasters look back at their first ever attempt at Web publishing with a mixture of pride and professional cringe. On the one hand they remember fondly their first efforts towards becoming fully conversant with online publishing. On the other hand, it is often too worrying just how many mistakes you can make the first time around.

Keep it simple

One of the biggest mistakes that new users make when putting together their first Web page is trying to stuff as many bells and whistles into a single site as possible. It is very tempting to show off, and put all the cool things you've seen at your favourite Web sites into your very own — things like flashing text, background music, animated icons, huge spinning 3D logos and headings, scrolling text, never-ending javascript announcements...the works.

One of the first things that experience teaches you is — don't go overboard.

The first time you see an animated email icon, it may look impressive. But the second, third, fourth time...? Avoid run-of-the mill Web site decorators, such as page counters (do your visitors really care how many other people have seen the site?), repetitive scrolling announcements, and "under construction" signs (it is accepted that Web pages are under perpetual refinement).

No one will be impressed with your "artistic talents" if your Web site is so overloaded with graphics and other gimmicks that it is impossible to use the site, or if it takes too long to download. Your Web site can be clever, imaginative and fun, but it should above all accomplish that primary purpose you decided on during the planning process. If that purpose is to showcase your skills as a designer, that's certainly legitimate. But if your design efforts, no matter how flashy and intricate, detract from communicating your message to your visitors, you've failed.

Beware proprietary designs

There are now a wide selection of graphic and other design tools available online, offering Web designers a myriad of options in terms of expressing themselves. But a few words of caution are in order.

Web browsers have limited support for graphic formats. In fact, you can only safely assume that users will be able to view JPEG and GIF images (we discuss these in Chapter 4). Beyond that, you might have some compatibility issues.

The standard solution for such compatibility problems is to provide "plug-ins" (special programs that enhance the capabilities of Web browsers) specifically designed to allow a Web browser to display, or otherwise, use specially created graphic and multimedia files. For example, Shockwave has become quite popular with Web designers who want to add some extra colour and excitement on their Web sites. Unfortunately, Web browsers do not support Shockwave file formats, with the result that users must download and install the Shockwave plug-in (www.macromedia.com/shockwave/) before they can view these animations.

Many users will object to having to spend an hour or so downloading special software for the sole purpose of watching your new, whiz-bang introductory screen. In fact, most won't bother. Of those who do, there will be a number who experience problems installing the plug-ins (they are far from easy to install and configure), meaning they can't view it even if they want to.

The best advice, then, is to avoid using special file formats altogether, unless all Web browsers support them as a native format.

It is a different issue altogether, of course, if the purpose of your Web site mandates the use of the special software. For instance, many Web sites offering online training courses use multimedia, such as Shockwave and QuickTime (www.quicktime.apple.com/). Other Web sites, such as news and cinema sites, offer users access to online video clips that they can view on their PCs. In such cases users would expect to download the appropriate software to view specially created multimedia animations.

Keep performance issues in mind

As mentioned in the section discussing bandwidth issues, it is important to remember that not everyone has the latest in PC technology. In fact, there are still large numbers of users who access the Internet with 486-based (and even 386-based) PCs, as well as older style Macintoshes, such as the Mac Classic. Indeed, there are still clusters of users who surf the Web with their much-cherished Amstrads, Commodores and Amigas.

You should take this diversity of PC hardware into consideration when designing your Web site. Although graphics might load quickly on your newer model PC, they might be a little tardier on slower machines.

Similarly, don't base the design of your Web site on the assumption that all viewers will have special hardware. For instance, many Web users (especially those who access the Internet from work) do not have soundcards installed, which prevents them from playing audio or music files. For this reason it would be quite foolish to design an "interactive" site in which all navigational prompts are supplied audibly.

Maintain browser neutrality. It's true that different Web browsers offer special features that can be used to make Web sites more attractive to certain users. However, you should not design your Web site with one Web browser in mind — after working so hard to design your Web site, why turn users away (or provide them with a substandard Web experience)? Most Web authoring packages can test your Web pages to ensure that they can be viewed correctly by all Web browsers. Be sure to take advantage of this feature.

If an area of your Web site takes a particularly long time to download, advise visitors of this. For example, if your site hosts an online catalogue, and has several high-resolution colour images of your products on each page, advise visitors that they can expect to wait, for example, 30 seconds each for the images to download. This will help stem attention loss, as well as assure visitors that their Web browser hasn't crashed or that your Web site isn't malfunctioning.

In the case of an online catalogue, a merchant selling, say, oil paintings, could display thumbnail previews of the paintings and appropriate text descriptions. These would download and be displayed on the visitor's screen quite quickly. The visitor could then be given the option of selecting which previews s/he wanted to see in full size.

Keep the object of the game in mind

Before adding any new bells and whistles to your site, ask yourself the following questions:

- ☐   Does the feature actually enhance communication with my visitors?
- ☐   Will the additional feature be compatible with all Web browsers?
- ☐   Are users required to download special software before the feature will work properly? If so, will downloading the software present any difficulties?
- ☐   Are there any obvious or potential compatibility or performance issues with the feature that I am planning?

The best course is to cater for the common denominator:

✗ Not everyone can view graphics when searching the Web (for example, a number of university students — who account for a large portion of the Internet user base — obtain Web access using network terminals that can only display monochrome text). Also, many Web users configure their Web browsers not to display Web graphics, so as to speed up Web site access. For this reason, make sure you provide a text-only alternative, or provide text-based navigation elements.

> If you plan to make use of a number of large image files, as in the case of an online catalogue, you might consider creating "thumbnail" images. Creating a thumbnail involves making a copy of the original image and saving it at a lower resolution and with smaller dimensions. The end result is a smaller image (in terms of both area and file size) that provides visitors with a "preview" of the original image.

✗ Not everyone has a high-speed computer, and may have difficulties in viewing large animation files.

✗ Not everyone has a high-speed modem. Users may become impatient waiting for files to download.

✗ Not everyone can, or wants to, listen to music while they browse.

✗ Not everyone will have all the plug-ins and other special software to take advantage of the latest and greatest multimedia trick.

✗ Not everyone will have the latest version Web browser.

Keep it fresh

One of the keys to encouraging visitors to return to your Web site time and again is to offer them new content. Update your Web site regularly by adding new content, and reworking existing content.

The frequency with which you update your content will depend, of course, on the nature of your Web site. For example, if your Web site is dedicated to following the progress of a famous golfer or football team, then you should expect to update your Web site at least once a week, possibly more often if games are played more frequently.

On the other hand, if your Web site is keeping track of the latest findings of a NASA probe, then you only need to update it each time there is a new report of an interesting finding.

At the other end of the spectrum, if you operate a stockbroking firm, and you use your Web site to keep clients informed of the stock exchange's performance, then your clients will be expecting hourly updates as a minimum.

Once you have finished creating your Web site, upload the files to the computer that will be hosting your Web site, so that you can test it for yourself, and make sure that there are no missing files, corrupted images or hyperlinks that do not work.

Once you are satisfied that your Web site looks and acts how you intended it to, invite a select group of friends to visit your Web site and critique it. Provide them with a checklist of the issues that you want them to test, such as:

- How quickly do the individual pages download?
- How do the graphics look?
- How legible is the text and graphics?
- Is the content appealing and interesting?
- Is the colour scheme and general design appealing?
- Do the navigational aides help or hinder?
- Is it easy to find specific material of interest on the site?
- Is the site consistent?

Ensure that users report all problems that they experience – they should not assume that any problem that they encounter is due to problems with their software etc. The feedback that you receive from this process is invaluable, and will help you design a genuinely useable and interesting Web site.

Conclusion

This chapter should have given you an insight into the process of designing your Web site and formulating its navigational elements and structure. Once you have completed this process, you are almost ready to begin creating your Web site. Hopefully you will also have picked up a few clues on common mistakes to be avoided.

There is one final step, however: creating or gathering suitable graphics to augment your Web site. The following chapter contains a quickie introduction to the world of graphics

Resources

Sun Guide to Web Style - www.sun.com/styleguide/

Web Developers Virtual Library - wdvl.internet.com

Yale Web Style Guide - info.med.yale.edu/caim/manual/

Web Pages that Suck - www.webpagesthatsuck.com

Web Page Design for Designers - www.wpdfd.com

Chapter 4

Graphics for Beginners

It is hard to imagine, but when the World Wide Web was first launched, it was very much a text-only affair. In those heady, early 90s (which seem like an eon ago for some), scientists and other academics primarily used the Web as a platform for distributing research data, scientific papers and journals. Most accessed it from computer terminals that could only display very simple text — images were useless.

Today, you cannot wander anywhere on the Web without seeing images. They are used to identify Web sites (company logos) and products (brand icons). Some Web sites use images for decoration, others incorporate images into their navigation systems so that users can move about the site with ease. Increasingly news and other information services are including photos and online video footage to illustrate the events in the world around us.

Everyone wants images!

This chapter shows you how to prepare your own images, including logos and banners. But first, it's useful to go over some technical terms and concepts.

Image formats

Before you start creating images you should be aware of the two main image formats used on the Web: JPEG and GIF. These are currently the only graphic formats that all Web browsers, on both Windows and Macintosh, can display without the need for special software. The bulk of the images that you will come across online will be either JPEG or GIF images (denoted, respectively, by the .jpg or .gif file extension)

JPEG, pronounced "jay-peg", stands for Joint Photographic Expert Group, the name of the standards group that created the format. JPEG image files use special data compression techniques, known as "lossy compression", to reduce the file size of a stored image. It is called "lossy" as some of the image data is lost in the compression process (but not enough to affect the overall quality of the image). GIF, pronounced either "jiff" or "giff" (depending on whom you ask), stands for

Graphics Interchange Format. It uses a "lossless" compression process, which means that all the data is preserved. As a result, GIF images tend to be larger than JPEG images.

Most image creation and editing programs support both of these formats (as well as many others) or provide the option of converting image files into these formats. Many also offer an "export" function, which allows you to save an existing image file in a different graphic format. For example, you might load and modify a GIF image, then export it to the JPEG format.

If your image-editing software doesn't provide a specific export function, you might be able to achieve the same result via the "Save As" option.

The JPEG image format is mainly used for digitised photographs and "continuous tone" images (that is, images that contain large areas of the same colours), which tend to stand up a little better to the data loss inherent in the compression process.

It is also preferable to the GIF format for photograph-quality images for one simple, but important, reason: GIF graphics are limited to a 256-colour palette (discussed below), whereas JPEG files can have a much larger number of colours.

The GIF image format (also commonly referred to as GIF89a, GIF87 or Compuserve GIF) is mainly used for indexed-colour (or flat colour) graphics — that is, those that use fewer or less-complex colours.

JPEG or GIF?

One of the key issues when preparing graphics for the Internet is file size — the smaller the better (see Chapter 10 on Bandwidth for a discussion of the issues raised by file sizes).

The smaller the size of the image file, the faster the visitor's Web browser can download and display it. Because of the different ways in which the two formats compress and store different types of images, it is not simply a matter of choosing one format and sticking to it. You will have to experiment, until you get a feel for which file format is better (in terms of both file size and image quality) for the types of images that you are creating.

Incidentally, when you save an image in JPEG format, most image creation software will give you the option of specifying what level of compression you want — in other words, how much you want to the software to "squash" the file.

Remember that the JPEG format uses "lossy compression", with the result that the higher the level of compression used, the lower the image quality of the saved file. When you are creating JPEG images for your Web site, you should experiment with different compression levels to find the best balance between image quality and size.

Save each image that you create in both formats, playing with the colour palettes (and the compression levels on JPEG files). This might seem tedious at first, but before long you will develop an understanding of the benefits and disadvantages of both formats.

Transparent and interlaced images

You might notice that your graphic creation program gives you the option of saving GIF files as either a transparent or an interlaced image (these options are only available with GIF images).

Ordinarily, GIF images are stored in a "linear" fashion: they are downloaded and displayed line by line (from the top of the image downwards). With larger files, it may take some time before the whole image is displayed, or at least before enough detail is available so that the user can ascertain what the image is.

An interlaced image is stored in a nonlinear manner, so that a Web browser can depict a blurry façade of the entire image in one pass. As more image data is downloaded, the image quality is sharpened, until the complete image is displayed.

Interlacing is handy when you cannot avoid larger images, but don't want users to become impatient during download. Those users who want to wait for the entire image to download can. Those who need only see enough of it before continuing on can.

Interlaced images are also useful when you have an image at the top of the page with text underneath. Web browsers will download enough of the image to display the façade, then download and display the text before retrieving the rest of the image data. Visitors don't have to wait for the full image to download before they can read the contents of the page — quite handy if your image is large.

A transparent image will let the background colour of a Web site show through in the GIF image whenever a specified colour — or no colour — is present in the image.

For example, say you created a rectangular banner that contained the word "Welcome" in red type on a blue background. Viewed by itself, the image looks fine. But when you place that image on a Web page that has a white background (or some colour other than blue), it looks "blocky" and doesn't integrate well with the overall appearance of the Web page.

Rather than create multiple banners with different background colours, you can save the image as a transparent GIF, with the blue background as the transparent area. Once you have done this, the background of the transparent GIF image will automatically match the background colour of your Web page. For instance, if you put the image — containing "Welcome" in red type on a blue, transparent background — on a Web page with a white background, the blue background will be displayed as white (therefore blending in). If you put the same image onto a Web page with a yellow background, the blue section will be displayed as yellow.

Not all image creation programs will allow you to save images as transparent GIFs, but most of the popular programs will. Colour transparency settings are generally only available when you are saving or exporting the image.

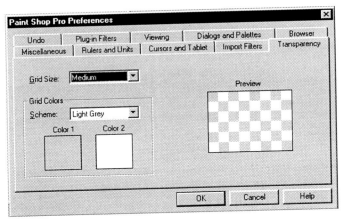

Paint Shop Pro allows users to specify the transparent colour for an image.

This Web page contains two copies of the same image.

The image on the left is not transparent. The image on the right is

Image resolution

The word "Resolution" describes the quality (in terms of sharpness and clarity) of a picture or image. The higher the resolution, the better the image quality. It's often measured in dots per inch of screen space (a dot is the smallest identifiable piece of an image), or "dpi". Therefore, the higher the dpi, the clearer and sharper the image.

The average computer monitor cannot display images at better than 72dpi resolution. Compared to print resolutions (for instance, most books and magazine images are printed at 2400dpi) this would seem quite poor. But 72dpi offers sufficient display quality for most images. Image creation programs will normally save images in a higher resolution (usually around 150 dpi to 300dpi), unless you specifically request that they be saved at a lower resolution. Given that higher resolutions mean larger files, and that those higher resolutions are wasted on most monitors, it doesn't make sense to save images at higher than 72dpi.

Image sizes

Image size is a vexing issue. On the one hand, the larger the image, the easier it is to see, and the more information it can contain. On the other hand, larger images lead to larger file size.

Here's some mathematics for you. The average computer monitor will display 640 x 480 pixels. So, a 200 x 200 pixel image will occupy around one-sixth of a 640 x 480 monitor. This might be a good size for your corporate logo (which you will want to display prominently), but it is a little too big for navigational icons — if they were this size, you'd soon run out of space for content! Of course, this exercise assumes that users will be viewing your Web site with their browsers set to display in "full screen". If their browser window is smaller than their full screen, the problem of crowding becomes even worse.

In addition to image resolution, you will need to play with image size (usually measured in pixels, but occasionally in millimetres or centimetres) to work out which size works best. Be sure that your images are legible (remember, not everyone has 20/20 eyesight), but that they do not dominate the screen excessively.

A pixel is actually comprised of three separate dots, but they are displayed so close together that they appear connected. As mentioned earlier, most standard sized monitors will display 600 x 480 pixels. So, if yours is a standard sized monitor, there are 480 vertical lines containing 600 pixels displayed horizontally across the viewable area of your computer screen — that should give you some idea of just how small pixels are!

Resources

Web Graphics on a Budget - www.mardiweb.com/web/

Creating Graphics for the Web - www.widearea.co.uk/designer/

Bozine Web Graphics Help - www.bozine.com/helppages.html

The Graphics Library - www.graphicslibrary.com

Developer Shed - www.devshed.com/resource.phtml

Chapter 5

Free Images for Your Web Site

Not everyone has the time, patience or inclination to create their own graphics. But this does not mean that your Web site is destined for a dreary appearance. There are plenty of Web sites available that host massive collections of free images (including animated icons) and other graphics.

When is free, free?

Before you get the wrong idea, this is probably a good time to explain the "etiquette" of image borrowing.

When someone creates an image for their site, whether it is a corporate logo or a simple little navigation button, they own that image, in that it is their creation and they retain the copyright to it. Therefore, as a general rule, it is not only wrong to "borrow" images from another Web site (no matter how generic they may appear), it may also be illegal. If you see an image on a Web site that you absolutely must have, your best bet is to email the Webmaster or owner of the Web site and ask whether you can take a copy for your Web site. In most cases, the individual will probably be flattered that you like the image so much!

If you really want to impress your customers, and keep them coming back, place less emphasis on snazzy Web design, and pay more attention to creating original, relevant content. Gee-whiz graphics are ten-a-penny. Well written, interesting content, however, is often hard to find.

Image warehouses

So although you should always be wary of borrowing images without permission, there are plenty of resources for free, public domain images.

Many Web sites, as mentioned above, are devoted to giving away copies of icons and other graphics. In such cases, there are no problems with downloading and using the images for your own Web site. You'll find hundreds of such sites online, with more graphics than you could ever use in a lifetime. Here are a few sites to get you on your way:

- **The Free Site** - www.thefreesite.com/freegraphics.htm
- **Xoom Free Clip Art** - xoom.com/xoom/web_clip_empire
- **Fantasyland Graphics** - www.enchantress.net/fantasy/index.shtml
- **Andy's Art Attack** - www.andyart.com
- **Free Art** - www.mcs.net/~wallach/freeart/buttons.html
- **Syruss's Graphics** - www.syruss.com
- **Icon Bazaar** - www.iconbazaar.com
- **Graphic Station** - www.graphicstation.com
- **Site Builder Gallery** - www.microsoft.com/gallery
- **Media Builder Library** - www.mediabuilder.com/graphicsfree.html

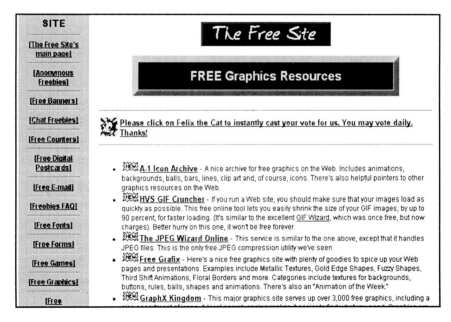

The Free Site provides links to many high quality images.

These are merely a sampling of the hundreds of sites offering free graphics for download. Find more for yourself at:

> http://www.yahoo.com/Arts/Design_Arts/Graphic_Design/
> Web_Page_Design_and_Layout/Graphics/Icons/

Free banners

Banners themselves are nothing more than large rectangular-ish graphics, and are pretty simple to make (as we demonstrated in the previous chapter). However, as they are often used for promoting your Web site or specific products and services, they tend to be very specific in terms of looks and content. (We discuss the process of banner advertising in Chapter 9, Promoting Your Web site). As such, it is unlikely that you will find any suitable banners in free Web collections.

But this does not mean that you have to do without. There are a number of Web sites that offer automated banner creation services: type in the words that you would like to appear in your banner, select from a range of different styles and, hey presto, a new banner.

For the sake of this example, we will use The Banner Generator (www.coder.com/creations/banner/) service, which is free for all users. However, there are a number of different banner creation sites (see the list below).

The Banner Generator Web site at www.coder.com/creations/banner/

The first step is to complete the Banner Generator Form, which you access via a link on the home page. Enter the text of your proposed banner, and select what graphic format you wish to create (GIF or JPEG) and what size you wish to make it. Each option has a help section, which can be accessed by clicking on the "?" symbol beside it.

Once you have specified the banner's contents, format and dimensions, your next task is to decide what style font you wish to use. There are a number to choose from and plenty of examples to help you make up your mind. You can then select what colour background and foreground you wish to use. Finally, you have the choice of several special effects. Again there are numbered examples to show you what each effect will produce.

---

coder.com   Creations Banner Activate Examples Fonts Docs Blanks

The Banner Generator Form

[Reload this Form] - [No Tables Form]

[?] Banner Text: `The text of my sample banner`

[?] Image Format: `gif` ▾   [?] Font Size: `30`   [?] Border: `5` × `5`

[?] Banner Quality: `Low` ▾   [?] Interlace: `No` ▾

[?] Font: Choose Font Family and Font Name.   [all samples]

- ○ Bitmapped Fonts: `AvantGarde-Book` ▾   [samples]
- ⦿ Standard Fonts: `CharterBT-Roman` ▾   [samples]
- ○ Hershey Fonts: `Hershey-Gothic-English` ▾   [samples]
- ○ Conservative Fonts: `FrutigerCndObl-Normal-Normal` ▾   [samples]
- ○ Longhand Fonts: `LeftyCasual` ▾   [samples]
- ○ Script Fonts: `Kaufmann` ▾   [samples]
- ○ Old Fonts: `FetteFraktur` ▾   [samples]
- ○ Caps Fonts: `Engraver-Light-Normal` ▾   [samples]
- ○ The Rest of the Fonts: `Frankfurt` ▾   [samples]

[Submit Banner]   [Reset]

[?] Foreground Color: `black` ▾   [?] rgb(color-list): `#rrggbb`

[?] Background Color: `white` ▾   [?] rgb(color-list): `#rrggbb`

[?] Transparency: `none` ▾   [?] Rotation: `Horizontal` ▾

***Enter the text to appear on your banner,
then select the font you wish to use.***

Once you have specified the parameters for the banner, click on the Submit Banner icon.

Within a few seconds you will be shown a screen confirming that your banner has been created, with information on how to view the banner. The final step in the process is saving the banner to your hard disk, which is discussed in the next section. Once you have done so, you might like to go back and start again, experimenting with the different options.

Making banners is EASY!

The final product

Saving graphics

Downloading and saving copies of images for your own use is quite a simple task. If you see a graphic that you would like to download, click on it with your right mouse button and select Save Picture As from the menu that appears. Mac users can access the same menu by clicking on the image and holding the mouse button down.

The Save Picture dialogue box will appear, allowing you to select the directory to which you want to save the file, as well as give it a meaningful name. You cannot, however, change its extension — it must remain .gif or .jpeg.

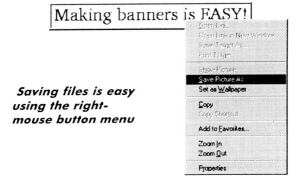

***Saving files is easy
using the right-
mouse button menu***

It is generally a good idea to store the images in the same directory as your other Web files – it makes them easier to manage and use.

Conclusion

There are a number of excellent sources of quality icons and graphics that you are free to use on your Web site. There are also a number of Web sites that will auto-mate the process of creating custom graphics.

Now that you have all the graphics that you need for your Web site, it is time to start constructing it. In the next chapter we will introduce you to HTML basics and Web authoring programs.

Resources

Instant Online Banner Creator - www.crecon.com/banners.html

MediaBuilder Animated Banner Maker - www.mediabuilder.com/abm.html

CoolBE - www.coolbe.com (downloadable banner creation software)

Four Corners Effective Banners - www.whitepalm.com/fourcorners/

Chapter 6

Hypertext Markup Language (HTML)

This chapter is designed as an introduction to HyperText Markup Language (HTML). Given the recent progress made in developing truly WYSIWYG (what-you-see-is-what-you-get), point-and-click Web authoring packages, few Web authors will actually have to bother themselves with the nitty-gritty of HTML. Even the greenest of Web authors can now compose professional-looking Web sites without having to write a single line of HTML. (We take a look at some of the most user-friendly Web authoring programs in the next chapter).

Even so, a broad understanding of HTML and its capabilities and limitations is of some benefit, especially if you find yourself wanting to take advantage of some of its more advanced features.

It's important to realise from the start that you do not control the ultimate look of your Web site: your visitors do, based on the preferences they set up in their browsers. For example, one visitor may prefer to use the font Times New Roman to display your Web site content, another might prefer Helvetica — a very different look. Yet another might have set the browser so that, in order to reduce loading time, it doesn't display graphics. One might keep the browser window small, while another might use the entire screen. All these preferences change the final appearance of your page on their computer. HTML allows you to specify within a reasonable margin how you want your page to look, but at the end of the day, the user visiting your site plays a major role in how it is actually viewed.

Even ignoring the other design issues raised earlier in this book, this aspect alone is reason enough to keep your Web site simple – a fair balance of graphics and well-spaced text.

HTML 101

The HyperText Markup Language is essentially a collection of commands - called tags — integrated into plain text documents that are interpreted by Web browsers. The tags themselves are not like ordinary computer "languages", in that they are plain English words or abbreviations. They are contained in angle-brackets

(< and >). Broadly speaking, tags are case-insensitive, so it doesn't matter whether you use upper or lower case, although you need to keep in mind that most tags come in pairs — such as the tag to begin boldface (**<B>**) and the tag to end boldface (**</B>**). Each tag of the pair must be in the same case. It is generally preferable to use uppercase for tags, as it makes them easier to find when you are manually editing HTML documents.

Each pair of tags has a beginning tag and an end tag (the end tag denoted by the use of the slash "/" character):

```
<TAG>
. . .
</TAG>
```

Most tags define what is to be done with the text between them. For example, all text encapsulated within the boldface tags (**<B>** and **</B>**) will be displayed in boldface on the viewer's computer screen.

It is important to use the tags in a structured way. This becomes quite imperative when you are designing Web pages that will be viewed by visitors using a number of possible types of Web browsers. It will also be a great help when you (or someone else) needs to go back to a document to update or revise it - something written in a bout of creativity might subsequently be incomprehensible at a later date.

As you start creating more advanced Web documents (such as using tables, for example) it may be impossible to avoid nesting tags; that is, using tags within tags. However, as a general rule, nested tags should be avoided. While nesting is not as great a problem with the latest Web browsers, earlier versions of different Web browsers often interpreted nested tags in different ways (often rendering Web pages unviewable to some).

For instance, the following sequence of tags:

```
<TAG1>
text
<TAG2>
more text
</TAG2>
</TAG1>
```

...might be interpreted in two different ways by two different Web browsers, with the result that your Web page might be displayed incorrectly on the viewer's computer screen. Also, by avoiding unnecessary nesting, your HTML documents are significantly easier to edit, revise and "troubleshoot".

Beware non-standard tags

Before we take a look at the basic HTML tags, a word of warning. Although there are agreed "standards" regulating the way in which HTML tags should be interpreted by Web browsers, the creators of various Web browser programs, especially Internet Explorer and Netscape Navigator/Communicator, have seen fit to develop their own, proprietary tags (that is, non-standard HTML tags that are only supported by their Web browser).

Where possible, you should avoid using non-standard HTML tags. By using only those tags accepted as standard by all Web browsers, you can be assured that your Web pages will be displayed properly on the viewer's computer screen, regardless of what computer or Web browser they are using.

> **To find out which tags are included in the "official" HTML standards, visit the World Wide Web Consortium Web site: (http://www.w3.org/).**

HTML Tags

Document tags

Document tags are used to identify the beginning and end of a Web page. They are also used to provide Web browsers with certain information about the Web page itself (for example, its title if it has one).

The <HTML> and </HTML> tags

The first line of every Web page should be the `<HTML>` tag. This simply indicates to Web browsers that it is the beginning of the page. The corresponding end tag is `</HTML>`, used at the very end of the document.

The content of a Web page is essentially broken up into two parts: the Head and the Body. Both parts are encompassed within `<HTML>` and `</HTML>`.

The <HEAD> and </HEAD> tags

The HEAD tags contain all of the document's header information. The header of a HTML document contains certain information used by Web browsers, such as the title of the document. Many browsing and search programs restrict themselves to the text within the `<HEAD>` and `</HEAD>` tags when performing a search, so you may want to take some thought for what you will enclose within them. For example, many designers include their page's title and introductory paragraph as part of the header information.

The <TITLE> and </TITLE> tags

This tag is usually used within the **<HEAD>** tags (although it's not mandatory). The title you specify within the **<TITLE>** and **</TITLE>** tags will be displayed in the Web browser's title bar, and, on certain Web browsers, will also appear in the history list (a record of sites the user has been to that can be accessed for easier navigation). When visitors add the Universal Resource Location (URL) of your Web site to their bookmark file, the bookmark's name will be whatever you have enclosed in the **<TITLE>** tags.

The <BODY> and </BODY> tags

The **<BODY>** and **</BODY>** tags enclose the actual "body" of your Web page: the text, graphics and links that will be displayed by the viewer's Web browser. The <**BODY>** start tag comes right after the **</HEAD>** end tag.

The basic outline of a Web page will look something like this (don't worry yet about the tags you don't know; they're explained below):

```
<HTML>
<HEAD>
<TITLE>My Sample Web Page</TITLE>
</HEAD>
<BODY>
 <H1>My First Web Page</H1>
 <P>
This is my first Web page.
 <P>
I think that I have some way to go before I get the hang of it all!
 <P>
 <HR>
</BODY>
</HTML>
```

My First Web Page

This is my first Web page.

I think that I have some way to go before I get the hang of it all!

***The above Web page as viewed with the Internet Explorer Web browser.
It also demonstrates the <HR> tag, discussed below.***

Tags for use within the body of a Web document

Heading tags

Heading tags (not to be confused with the header information tags `<HEAD>` and `</HEAD>`) are used to emphasise text within a HTML document by changing the size and putting the text in somewhat heavier type. There are six different headings sizes, numbered 1 to 6, with 1 being the largest. The heading tags are used in pairs. For example:

`<H1>`Heading 1`</H1>`

`<H2>`Heading 2`</H2>`

`<H3>`Heading 3`</H3>`

`<H4>`Heading 4`</H4>`

`<H5>`Heading 5`</H5>`

`<H6>`Heading 6`</H6>`

> # Heading 1
> ## Heading 2
> ### Heading 3
> Heading 4
>
> Heading 5
>
> Heading 6

The above heading tag example as viewed with a Web browser. Each heading appears on its own line; you cannot have two headings on one line.

The line break tag `<BR>`

HTML ignores any carriage returns or extra spaces. You must explicitly designate where you want new lines or blank lines. The line break tag, `<BR>`, forces the next line or word to start on a new line. (There is no corresponding `</BR>` tag, as there is really no such thing as the end of a line break!)

The paragraph tag `<P>`

Strictly speaking, each paragraph of text is enclosed within paragraph tags: `<P>` and `</P>`. Each time the paragraph tag appears, it instructs the Web browser to skip a line, so that the paragraphs have a bit of space between them. In practice, most people just use the paragraph start tag (`<P>`) each time they want a blank line between two pieces of text, and let the browser assume the end tag.

The paragraph tags can also be used to align text to the left, right or centre of the viewer's screen, by inserting an `"ALIGN="` statement. The modified tags look like this:

`<P ALIGN=LEFT>` aligns a paragraph to the left

`<P ALIGN=RIGHT>` aligns a paragraph to the right

`<P ALIGN=CENTER>` centres a paragraph

Note that HTML requires the American spelling of "center".

The <BLOCKQUOTE> and </BLOCKQUOTE> tags

The blockquote tags indent text, and are usually used to emphasise quoted text. Blockquote tags can be used in conjunction with other tags, such as the boldface tag (see below), or nested within tags, such as the paragraph tags.

Whenever the blockquote tag is used, the quoted text is placed on a new line (that is, there is an implicit line break, just as with the heading tags).

The list tags

Lists are fun, and quite handy. They can be used to make points stand out from other text (for example, when you are summarising the advantages of your products and services).

There are three basic types of lists: ordered, unordered and definition. The first two are quite similar and very easy to use. Definition lists are set up in a different fashion.

The ordered list tags: <OL> and </OL>

Ordered list tags are used when you want to use a numbered sequence in conjunction with your text. The ordered list tags instruct the Web browser to mark each point with an automatically generated, sequential number.

The `<OL>` tag marks the beginning of the listed items, and not surprisingly the `</OL>` tag marks the end. Each item in the list is marked using the `<LI>` ("List Item") tag. The `<LI>` tag has a corresponding `</LI>` tag, but this closing tag is not required to designate the end of the item, and most people don't bother using it.

As an example of using an ordered list, suppose you want to itemise the various resources available on your site:

```
<OL>
<LI>HTML tutorials
<LI>Links to free software
<LI>My favourite sites
<LI>Some fun sites
</OL>
```

```
1.  HTML tutorials
2.  Links to free software
3.  My favourite sites
4.  Some fun sites
```

The ordered list tag will allow you to automatically number your list points.

As the picture shows, when the list above is displayed on the user's screen, a sequential number will precede each article. But why bother with the extra tags when you could simply (and manually) number each item? It makes for easier editing. If you wanted to add extra items to a list you had already set up using ordered list tags, you could insert new items without having to manually renumber them: a significant time saver.

Unordered lists

If you use a word processor, you are probably familiar with the term "bulleted lists": each item is placed on a separate line and preceded by a small graphic, such as a circle or diamond. Bulleted lists can be achieved with HTML using the unordered list tags, **<UL>** and **</UL>**, in the same way as the ordered lists tags.

<UL>

<LI>HTML tutorials

<LI>Links to free software

<LI>My favourite sites

<LI>Some fun sites

</UL>

Instead of the article titles being preceded by a number, a "bullet" (most browsers use a small, solid circle) precedes each article.

Definition lists

This is where things get a little tricky! Definition lists do not number or otherwise manipulate text based upon sequence. Instead, they are used to group pairs of text items. For instance, you might want each article title to be followed by a brief description. To do this, you could use the definition list tags: **<DL>** and **</DL>** to begin and end the list, **<DT>** to specify the first item in a pair, and **<DD>** to specify the second item (or "definition"). Here's an example:

<DL>

<DT>HTML tutorials

<DD>Links to some cool online tutorials

<DT>Links to free software

```
<DD>Some of the best software around
<DT>My favourite sites
<DD>Where I like to hang out
<DT>Some fun sites
<DD>The Web isn't all work with no play
</DL>
```

> HTML tutorials
>   Links to some cool online tutorials
> Links to free software
>   Some of the best software around
> My favourite sites
>   Where I like to hang out
> Some fun sites
>   The Web isn't all work with no play

Using the definition list tags, you can pair sections of text together.

Changing text attributes using style tags

In the same way that you can highlight words in your word processor using underline, boldface and italics, you can highlight words in HTML using the style tags shown below.

The bold face tags

Everything between `<B>` and `</B>` tags is bold faced (that is, darkened text).

The italics tags

Everything between `<I>` and `</I>` tags is italicised.

The underline tags

Everything between `<U>` and `</U>` tags is underlined. You should be aware that few designers use the underline tags. Browsers often designate links with underlined text, and to have underlined text that does not function as a link can be confusing and frustrating to your visitors.

Here is an example of using style tags:

```
<B> This section of text  should appear in BOLD </B>
<BR>
<I> This section of text should appear in ITALICS </I>
<BR>
<U> This section of text should appear UNDERLINED </U>
```

This example looks like this when displayed with a Web browser:

> **This section of text should appear in BOLD**
> *This section of text should appear in ITALICS*
> This section of text should appear <u>UNDERLINED</u>

The style tags are used to change the appearance of text.

The font size & colour tags

In addition to using standard text formatting, you can change the size and colour of your text using the `<FONT SIZE>` and `<FONT COLOR>` tags.

For instance, the `<FONT SIZE=4>` tag would create text twice as large as the `<FONT SIZE=2>` tag. Because the HEADER tags require that header text appear on its own line, many users prefer to create headlines and headings using the `<FONT SIZE>` tag, to give them an option of whether it must appear on a separate line or not. Experiment with different values for SIZE= to get an idea of what you can achieve with font sizes, e.g.

`<FONT SIZE=5>`This text should be quite large`</FONT>`

You can change the colour of the displayed text using the `<FONT COLOR>` tag (note the American spelling of "color"). While there are a large number of possible colours that you can use in conjunction with this tag, not all are universally supported by all Web browsers. Commonly supported colours are: blue, white, cyan, black, fuchsia, and magenta, e.g.

`<FONT COLOR=fuchsia>`This text is the colour of fuchsia`</FONT>`

For a more detailed list of potential colours, visit www.netspot.unisa.edu.au/html/compendium/colors.htm

The horizontal rules tag `<HR>`

Horizontal rules are a handy way of dividing different parts of your HTML document. A horizontal rule is exactly what the name suggests — a ruled "line" across the screen that automatically extends the full width of the browser window.

Creating links between sites or other documents

Almost every Web site you will visit includes links to other related sites, or to separate Web pages within the same site. These links are generated using HTML anchor tags.

Anchor tags <A> and </A>

The anchor tags are used in conjunction with several different commands, depending on what you want to do.

The HREF command

The most common anchors used are in the form **<A HREF=**"URL"**>**, where URL is the Universal Resource Location (or Internet address) of the site, document or other resource to which you wish to create a link. HREF is an acronym for "Hypertext REFerence".

For example, you might advise visitors to your site to download the latest copy of your favourite game. You can include a link on your site such as:

    <A HREF="http://www.sierra.com/"**>**The Sierra Web site**</A>**

The text between the open and close anchor ("The Sierra Web site") will be displayed in a different colour or underlined (depending on how each visitor's Web browser is configured), indicating that it is a hyperlink. By clicking on the link with the mouse, visitors will be automatically connected to Sierra's home page, where they can download copies of the latest games.

When you want to direct the reader to a new page or a different HTML document on your site (as distinct from someone else's site), use the same command tags, but replace the URL with the directory path and name of the document. For example:

    <A HREF="nextpage.html"**>**Click here to move to the next page…**</A>**

Anchor tags can also be used to create a link on your Web site to your email address, so that visitors can send you email. By inserting a "mailto." command, visitors can click on it to open their favourite email program with a blank email message already addressed to you.

The mailto tag works like this:

    <A HREF="mailto:your email address"**>**Click here to send me email**</A>**

For example, if I wanted to include a mailto link on my Web site, I would use the command:

`<A HREF =`"mailto:mpn@bigpond.com"`>` Click here to send me email`</A>`

Linking to a specific place on a Web document

Sometimes Web sites are set up as one single page, to make printing their contents easier for browsers. A recipe book, for example, can have an index at the top of a page, with all the recipes following consecutively. Rather than require readers to scroll through a long Web page (remember, most users won't scroll!!), you can insert a series of "anchor" hyperlinks, which allow users to jump to a particular section of a single Web document.

The tag is very similar to the plain hyperlinks, but this time instead of pointing to a URL or a separate Web document, the tag points to another tag, the "Name tag".

To continue with our recipe example, the list of links at the top of the Web page would contain pointers to the various recipe types. The specific tags would look like this:

`<A HREF=`"#start"`>`Starters`</A>`
`<A HREF=`"#entree"`>`Entree`</A>`
`<A HREF=`"#main"`>`Main Meals`</A>`
`<A HREF=`"#dessert"`>`Dessert`</A>`

As you can see, these point to areas of the document titled "#start", "#entrée" etc. In the document itself, there would be corresponding tags:

`<A NAME=`"start"`>`Starters`</A>`

`<p>` Here is a selection of mouth watering starters to suit all lifestyles and budgets. They are divided into meat categories first then vegetarian dishes. Take your time and enjoy our fabulous recipes. `</p>`
`<A NAME=`"dessert"`>`Dessert `</A>`
… etc.

And now for some pretty pictures ...

Life would be pretty boring without colour. Similarly, a Web site would be fairly unattractive without graphics. HTML has the answer for this too.

The IMG Tag: <IMG>

Like the anchor tags, the `<IMG>` tag is used in conjunction with other commands. (Unlike the anchor tags, it stands alone: there is no `</IMG>` end tag.)

Primarily, it is used in conjunction with the SRC (Source) command, which instructs Web browsers where to retrieve the image file for display:

`<IMG SRC="name of Graphic File">`

For example, if the image file (ball.gif) is in the same directory as the document that contains the link, your command would look like this:

`<IMG SRC="ball.gif">`

Alternatively, if you borrow a graphic image from another site, you have the option of downloading and saving your own copy, or including a link to it in your Web document. In the latter case, you would put in its full URL, such as:

`<IMG SRC="http://www.example.com/graphics/ball.gif">`

When the user's Web browser is loading your Web page, it will grab a copy from the other Web site and include it in yours.

IMG Tag attributes

There are a number of attributes that you can use in conjunction with the IMG tag, which modify its operation.

The ALT tag

Unfortunately, not every Internet user has access to a fully functioning Web browser capable of displaying images. Some may only have access to a system with no ability to display graphics. Other people specifically configure their Web browsers not to display images, as this makes searching for information much faster.

When users cannot see images, the comment [IMAGE] is substituted for the actual image, to indicate than an image would normally occupy the space marked. The ALT Tag is used to display alternative text for those who cannot, or choose not to, view images. These alternate descriptions are not used or displayed by browsers which can display graphics. For example:

`<IMG SRC="arrow.gif" ALT="Click Here to Continue">`

The ALIGN tag

As with the paragraph tags, you can use the `<IMG>` tag to align your images on the computer screen by inserting the `ALIGN=` tag.

For example:

`<IMG ALIGN=LEFT SRC="ball.gif">` places the image to the far left side of the screen.

`<IMG ALIGN=RIGHT SRC="ball.gif">` places the image to the far right side of the screen.

`<IMG ALIGN=CENTER SRC="ball.gif">` centres the image.

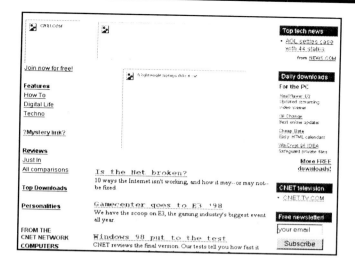

The C/Net Web site (www.cnet.com) minus its graphics...

and the same site with graphics

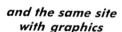

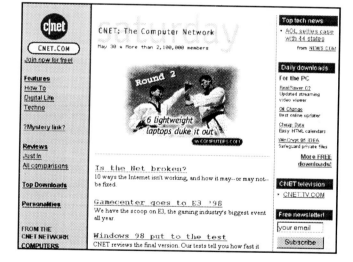

The HEIGHT and WIDTH tags

The HEIGHT and WIDTH tags specify the dimension of the image (in pixels). Although it is not compulsory that you specify each image's dimensions, it is a good idea to do so, as it helps the visitor's Web browser calculate how much space to leave on the screen for an image that it is yet to download.

e.g. `<IMG SRC="ball.gif" WIDTH=50 HEIGHT=30>`

If you specify pixel dimensions that are larger than the actual dimensions of the image, the Web browser will magnify the image. Conversely, if you specify dimensions that are smaller than the actual image, the Web browser will shrink it. Many Web designers use this to their advantage, purposely creating images that are smaller than necessary (which makes their file sizes smaller, and therefore they download faster), but use these tags to "scale" them up.

The VSPACE and HSPACE tags

The VSPACE and HSPACE tags are used to specify the amount of screen space that should be left between an image and the text/image appearing above or below or to the left or right of it.

E.g. `<IMG SRC="ball.gif" VSPACE=50 HSPACE=30>`

Put them altogether

Inserting an image making use of all these features is a bit longwinded, but it is an excellent way of maintaining control over just how your image is displayed by the Web browser:

`<IMG SRC="ball.gif" ALIGN=left HSPACE=10 ALT="Click to proceed to the next page" WIDTH=50 HEIGHT=30 VSPACE=10 HSPACE=10>`

Background colours

The default background colour for Web pages on most browsers is a light shade of grey, which is practical but not very appealing. Luckily, HTML allows you to easily change the default colour to something a little more aesthetically pleasing. You do this by inserting the `BGCOLOR=` command within the `<BODY>` tag.

The modified tag would look something like this:

`<BODY BGCOLOR="blue">` (note, again, the American spelling of "color")

There are quite a few colours that you can use within the `<BODY>` tag, including blue, yellow, white, red and black.

Background images

Many people feel that the choice of background colours, although broad, is restrictive. To remedy this problem, HTML also allows for background images. Instead of using a block of colour as a background, Web pages can display an image.

The background image can be a discernable image, such as a logo or picture of a product. This is a great way of "branding" your Web page as belonging to your or your company. Alternatively, the background image might simply be a special colour or a subtle pattern, created for the sole purpose of creating a custom background.

In either case, make sure that the background image is not overly large, as this will add to the total "size" of your Web site (in download terms). It should also be subtle enough that visitors will be able to easily discern the actual text of the site. A busy or brightly-coloured background image can make a Web page completely unreadable.

The command for using background images, which again is inserted within the **<BODY>** tag, is **BACKGROUND=**"name of image file".

For example:

```
<BODY BACKGROUND="logo.gif">
```

Making comments within documents

Occasionally you might want to make comments or leave reminder notes for yourself in a HTML document. For example, you might be rearranging your graphics or trying a new "trick", in which case it is a good idea to leave a message explaining what you are doing for future reference. This can be done using an exclamation point within the tag:

```
<! This is my comment.  >
```

The text "This is my comment" will not be displayed on the user's screen.

Tables

Many people regard the availability of tables in HTML as something of a Godsend. Tables, after all, give authors fairly exacting control over how images and text appear on the page. Unfortunately, this has led to the abuse and misuse of tables.

The tables tags were designed to allow information to be displayed in a tabular format (such as spreadsheets, timetables and the like). But users quickly discovered that they could also be used to space graphics and text quite accurately.

Tables can certainly help jazz up your Web designs, as they allow for some fairly imaginative page layouts. But before you jump into using tables with both feet, it pays to warn that **not** all tables are created equally – yes, browsers do interpret some tables' tags differently. And when it comes to tables (as you will no doubt find out) even minor display variations can change the intended effect.

So, suitably warned, let's take a look at the basic table tags.

Overview

Tables are a means of arranging text and images into "rows", "cells" and "columns" (these concepts should be familiar to those who use spreadsheet programs).

	Column 1	Column 2	Column 3	Column 4
Row 1				
Row 2		Cell 2,2		
Row 3				Cell 4,3
Row 4	Cell 1,4			

There are three main tags used to create tables:

Table tags: **<TABLE>** and **</TABLE>**
Row tags: **<TR>** and **</TR>**
Cell tags: **<TD>** and **</TD>**

The general rule of thumb when it comes to tables is that the **<TD>** & **</TD>** tags are used within the **<TR>** and **</TR>** tags, which in turn are "wrapped" within the **<TABLE>** and **</TABLE>** tags.

The easiest way to plan and create a table in HTML is to first visualise (or draw) how the table should look. Here is a basic table diagram, containing four cells in two rows, making 2 columns:

Cell 1,1   Cell 2,1
Cell 1,2   Cell 2,2

The HTML to achieve this is quite straight forward:

```
<table>
     <tr>
 <td>Cell 1,1</td>
 <td>Cell 2,1</td>
   </tr>
     <tr>
  <td>Cell 1,2</td>
 <td>Cell 2,2</td>
   </tr>
</table>
```

The data that appears in the individual cells is encapsulated within the **<TD>** tags, which are encapsulated within the individual **<TR>** tags.

If you want your table to stand out on the screen, you can use borders (so that lines appear between each row, column and cell). To add a border, use the **BORDER=** tag within the **<TABLE>** tag. Default border thickness is indicated by **BORDER=1**. You can vary the border width by increasing the value.

e.g. **<TABLE BORDER=3>**

To omit the borders altogether, set the tag to zero.

e.g. **<TABLE BORDER=0>**

Let's have a look at a different style table (this time with three rows and three columns):

```
<table border=2>
<caption> A simple table </caption>
 <tr>
          <th> Column 1 </th>
          <th> Column 2 </th>
          <th> Column 3 </th>
 </tr>
 <tr>

          <td> Number One </td>
          <td> Number Two </td>
          <td> Number Three </td>
 </tr>
 </table>
```

A simple table

Column 1	Column 2	Column 3
Number One	Number Two	Number Three

A simple, but effective table

You will notice that we used a new tab, **<TH>**. This works in essentially the same way as the **<TD>** tab, except that the encapsulated text is treated as a heading.

Another alternative for making text stand out within your table is to use the **<CAPTION>** tag. The table shown below uses both the **<TH>** and **<CAPTION>** tags.

```
<HTML><HEAD>
<TITLE>Roster for School Canteen</TITLE>
</HEAD><BODY><table border=2>
<caption> Canteen Roster, Week Ending 17.4.98 </caption>
<tr>
            <th> <br> </th>
            <th> Monday </th>
            <th> Tuesday </th>
            <th> Wednesday </th>
            <th> Thursday </th>
            <th> Friday </th>
</tr><tr>
            <th> 8am </th>
            <td> Mary </td>
            <td> Tanya </td>
            <td> Rebekah </td>
            <td> Peta </td>
            <td> Raegan </td>
</tr><tr>
            <th> 10am </th>
            <td> Tanya </td>
            <td> Rebekah </td>
            <td> Peta </td>
            <td> Raegan </td>
            <td> Mary </td>
</tr><tr>
            <th> 12pm </th>
            <td> Rebekah </td>
            <td> Peta </td>
            <td> Raegan </td>
            <td> Mary </td>
            <td> Tanya </td>
</tr></table></BODY></HTML>
```

Canteen Roster, Week Ending 17.4.98

	Monday	Tuesday	Wednesday	Thursday	Friday
8am	Mary	Tanya	Rebekah	Peta	Raegan
10am	Tanya	Rebekah	Peta	Raegan	Mary
12pm	Rebekah	Peta	Raegan	Mary	Tanya

Tables were designed to assist Web authors display information in tabular form.

The above text and examples pretty well cover the basics of tables (see, it wasn't that hard). But there are still a number of refinements and special attributes available.

If you only want your table to fill part of the screen, you can control its width and height with the **WIDTH=x** and **HEIGHT=x** attributes (set within the **<TABLE>** tag), where x is measured in pixels.. These attributes can be used in conjunction with other attributes, including **BORDER=x**, which, as we mentioned earlier, sets the thickness of the table's borders.

Example:

```
<table width=400 border=5>
<caption> A simple table </caption>
 <tr>
          <th> Column 1 </th>
          <th> Column 2 </th>
          <th> Column 3 </th>
 </tr>
 <tr>
          <td> Number One </th>
          <td> Number Two </td>
          <td> Number Three </td>
 </tr>
</table>
```

A simple table

Column 1	Column 2	Column 3
Number One	Number Two	Number Three

A similar style of table, but this time using borders and a width setting.

Example:

```
<table border=3>
<caption> A simple table </caption>
 <tr>
          <th width=120> Column 1 </th>
          <th width=200> Column 2 </th>
          <th width=60> Column 3 </th>
 </tr><tr>
          <td> Number One </th>
          <td> Number Two </td>
          <td> Number Three </td>
 </tr></table>
```

A simple table

Column 1	Column 2	Column 3
Number One	Number Two	Number Three

Use the WIDTH= attribute to create columns of varying sizes.

In addition to determining the perimeter of your table, you can control the spacing between the individual cells themselves, as well as the space between a cell's content (e.g. text or image) and the inner frame of the cell. This is achieved with the **CELLSPACING=x** and **CELLPADDING=x** attributes, which are also used within the **<TABLE>** tag.

Example:

```
<table cellspacing=10 border=3>
<caption> A simple table </caption>
 <tr>
            <th> Column 1 </th>
            <th> Column 2 </th>
            <th> Column 3 </th>
 </tr>

 <tr>
            <td> Number One </th>
            <td> Number Two </td>
            <td> Number Three </td>
 </tr>
</table>
```

A simple table

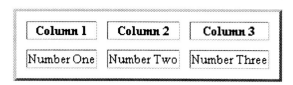

You can control the thickness of the boarder and the space between the individual cells.

Example:

```
<table cellpadding=20 border=3>
<caption> A simple table </caption>
 <tr>
          <th> Column 1 </th>
          <th> Column 2 </th>
          <th> Column 3 </th>
 </tr>
 <tr>
          <td> Number One </th>
          <td> Number Two </td>
          <td> Number Three </td>
 </tr>
</table>
```

A simple table

Column 1	Column 2	Column 3
Number One	Number Two	Number Three

Thicker "padding" between the cells makes their contents easier to read.

You can also take steps to position your table in a specific position on the screen using the **ALIGN=** attributes. The main attribute settings are left and right and center. You can centre your table as a whole, however this is achieved using the generic **<CENTER>** and **</CENTER>** tags.

Finally, you can also specify the alignment of data within a cell, using the **ALIGN=** attribute within the **<TD>** or **<TH>** tags (in conjunction with the left, right or center settings). You can also use **VALIGN=** attribute, in conjunction with the top, middle and bottom settings, to control the vertical alignment of text.

Example:

```
<center>
<table width=400 height=100 border=4>
<caption> A simple table </caption>
 <tr>
```

```
        <th align=right> Column 1 </th>
        <th align=center> Column 2 </th>
        <th align=left> Column 3 </th>
    </tr>

    <tr>
        <td align=right valign=top> Number One </th>
        <td align=center valign=middle> Number Two </td>
        <td align=left valign=bottom> Number Three </td>
    </tr>
</table>
```

A simple table

Column 1	Column 2	Column 3
Number One	Number Two	Number Three

***The ALIGN= attribute can also be used to manipulate
the position of your text.***

There are a number of other attributes and tags available for use with tables, but they are beyond the scope of a book such as this. See the resources listed at the end of this chapter for pointers to information about advanced table functions.

Conclusion

This chapter should give you sufficient understanding of the basics of HTML to be able to create your first Web site by hand, or fine tune a Web site created using a Web authoring program. Below is a list of online resources for those interested in learning more about HTML, or some of the more advanced HTML features such as tables and frames.

Resources

WebMonkey Tutorials - www.hotwired.com/webmonkey/html/

Web Reference - www.webreference.com

The Advanced HTML Reference - www.blooberry.com/html/

Guide to HTML & Forms - www.2kweb.net/guide-to-publishing-html

DJ Quad's Ultimate HTML Site - www.quadzilla.com

CoolZine's HTML Guide - coolzine.com/html/

HTML & Web Site Resource Page - www.library.carleton.edu/learnhtml

HTML Goodies - www.htmlgoodies.com

Compendium of HTML Elements - www.htmlcompendium.org/index.htm

HTML Help - www.htmlhelp.com

For an exhaustive list of HTML tutorials and guides, visit:
www.yahoo.com/Computers_and_Internet/Information_and_Documentation/
Data_Formats/HTML/Guides_and_Tutorials/

To Frame or Not to Frame

The use of frames on a Web site is a much-debated topic. Frames were developed to allow Web designers to "carve" the screen into two or more sections, and then design/code each section individually. Most people use frames for either navigational or advertising purposes. For example, a narrow frame is created down the left side or across the top of the screen, which is used to display either the navigational icons or persistent banner ads. This frame is displayed constantly, while the remainder of the screen changes depending on which areas of the Web site the visitor explores.

The authors are of the view that frames make for poor Web design, and as such do not cover them in this book. There are a number of reasons why you should not use frames, such as:

They create unnecessary complexity - both in terms of designing the Web site and navigating around it;

They can occasionally alter the user's Web browser preferences, especially in terms of image-loading;

They make the Web page loading time appear faster (and can add to the download time, as the Web browser has to download two or more HTML files at a time to create a single screen of information).

Frames are not universally supported, and many Frames implementations are browser-specific.

Finally, if these are not reason enough to avoid frames, then perhaps the fact that most users detest frames will convince you!

Chapter 7

HTML Examples

In the previous chapter, we took a look at the basic HTML tags that you are likely to use if you are "hand-coding" your first Web page (we look at some more user-friendly point-n-click Web editing solutions in the following chapter).

While the preceding HTML chapter is a handy ready-reference, you don't really get a feel for how HTML works until you see a few actual Web documents, and start picking individual portions apart. In this chapter, we've created a series of basic Web pages, which are displayed both in their raw HTML format and as screenshots so you can see how they appear when viewed with a Web browser. Each Web document is accompanied by a running commentary, to help you make sense of it all.

A "favourite links" Web site

Many people use their very first attempt at Web authoring to create a Web site containing a list of their favourite Web resources for their friends and online associates. These types of Web sites are very easy to create, as you will soon see.

Below is the HTML code for a fictional Web site: Lucy's Web Page. For ease of commentary, we have put each tag usage on a separate line. However, Web browsers do not recognise standard line breaks (only those inserted with the <BR> tag), so it wouldn't matter of you used more than one tag on a line, or had all of the HTML below on a single line!

```
<HTML>
<HEAD>
<TITLE>Lucy's Web Page</TITLE>
</HEAD>
<!— Here we are specifying colours throughout the document—>
<BODY bgcolor="#Black" text="#White" link="#Teal">
<center>
<p>
<font size=5 color="#Fuchsia">
<IMG SRC="squiggle.gif">
<!— We are creating some extra space between the image and the text
by making our text the same colour as the background, therefore
making it unreadable to users.—>
```

```
<font color="#Black"> aaaaaaaa </font color>
<B>Hi!</B>
<font color="#Black"> aaaaaaaa </font color>
<IMG SRC="squiggle.gif">
<BR>
My name is <B>Lucy</B>
<BR>
This is my web page of favourite links. </font size>
<HR width=50% size=8>
<BR>
<BR>
<p>
<font size=3>
<B>SPORTS LINKS</B>
</font size>
<BR>
<A HREF="http://www.nhl.com/">NHL Ice Hockey</a>
<BR>
<A HREF="http://www.sky.co.uk/manu/">Manchester United Soccer Team</a>
</p>
<BR>
<BR>
<p>
<font size=3>
<B>HEALTH LINKS</B>
</font size>
<BR>
<A HREF="http://www.charliechan.com/fran.html">Internet Yoga School</a>
<BR>
<A HREF="http://www.zero1zero.com.au/AOS/index.asp">Aerobics Oz Style</a>
</p>
<BR>
<p>
<font size=3>
<B>SOFTWARE LINKS</B>
</font size>
<BR>
<A HREF="http://www.microsoft.com/">Tucows</a>
<BR>
<A HREF="http://www.apple.com">Macintosh Software</a></p>
<BR>
<BR>
<p>
<font size=3>
```

```
<B>ASSORTED LINKS</B>
</font size>
<BR>
<A HREF="http://www.net-works.co.uk">Net.Works website</a>
<BR>
<A HREF="http://www.yahoo.com">Yahoo</a>
<BR>
<A HREF="http://www.hoyts.com.au">Hoyts</a>
</p></center></BODY></HTML>
```

How our HTML looks through the eyes of a Web browser.

A basic Small Business Web page

This is a very basic layout that demonstrates how to use the table tags to format a Web page layout. The Web page contains a **mailto:** link so that visitors can contact Julie's staff instantly with orders or requests for further information.

If this were a "live" site, the bulleted list of tasty treats could be displayed as hyperlinks, with links to other sections of the Web site containing images of the final product and pricing details.

Julie's Bakery

MISSION STATEMENT

Julie's Bakery aims to provide our customers with the finest, freshest food
We aim to satisfy even the fussiest of tastebuds and offer a full guarantee of quality on all our food.

Satisfaction or your money back!

Just a small selection of the tasty treats we offer are

- Fresh Bread and Scones
- Chocolate Mud Cakes
- Pastries - Sweet, Custard Tarts, Matchsticks etc.
- Pastries - Savoury, Pies, Sausage Rolls, Pasties etc.
- Cakes for all Occasions

Thankyou for visiting our site

This site is maintained and updated by Julie
Last modified 30th May, 1998.

Create a clean, fresh layout with the minimum of fuss using tables.

```
<HTML><HEAD><TITLE>Julie's Bakery</TITLE></HEAD>
<BODY bgcolor="White">

<!—The table forms the basis of our page layout. All images and
text are contained within table elements—>
<table cellpadding=10 border=0>
 <tr width=180 valign=top>
     <td> <IMG SRC="bread.jpg" width=150> </td>
     <td> <BR><IMG SRC="julie.gif" width=350></td>
 </tr>
 <tr width=180 valign=top>
     <td><BR><IMG SRC="cakes.jpg" width=150> <BR><BR><BR>
         <IMG SRC="cookies.jpg" width=150> </td>
<td><BR> <B>MISSION STATEMENT</B> <BR><BR>
Julie's Bakery aims to provide our customers with the finest, freshest
food.<BR> We aim to satisfy even the fussiest of tastebuds and offer a full
guarantee of quality on all our food.<BR><BR>
<B><I>Satisfaction or your money back!</I></B>
<p> Just a small selection of the tasty treats we offer are:

<!—Here is an unordered list,no need to close the <LI> tag—>
<UL>
<LI> Fresh Bread and Scones
<LI> Chocolate Mud Cakes
```

```
<LI> Pastries - Sweet; Custard Tarts, Matchsticks etc.
<LI> Pastries - Savoury; Pies, Sausage Rolls, Pasties etc.
<LI> Cakes for all Occasions
</UL>

<BR><BR><BR>
<center>
<I>Thankyou for visiting our site</I>
<BR> <BR>
<!—This is where browsers have the opportunity to email directly
from the site—>
```
This site is maintained and updated by
```
<A HREF="mailto:juliesbakery@bakers.co.uk">Julie</a><BR>
```
Last modified 30th May, 1998.
```
</center></td></tr></table></BODY></HTML>
```

Small Car Enthusiasts Web site

This site features a modest main graphic on the opening screen, some text and four navigational icons used to provide links to other areas within the site. Again, it is a fairly simple design. The focus of this page is to welcome visitors and direct them to specific areas of interest within the site. At the bottom of the screen is a general invite for visitors to contact the site's owner with any questions or queries.

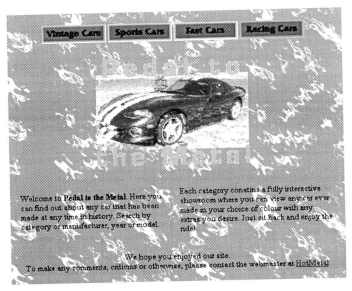

A Web page featuring several internal links for exploration.

```
<HTML><HEAD><TITLE>Pedal to the Metal</TITLE></HEAD>

<!—Our image "ripple.gif" will be tiled right across the background.
As such, there is no need for a background colour—>

<BODY background="ripple.gif" text="#Black">
<BR><BR><center>
<A  HREF="vintage.htm"><IMG  SRC="vintage.gif"  width=100  border=0
alt="Vintage Cars"></A>
<A HREF="sports.htm"><IMG SRC="sports.gif" width=100 border=0 alt="Sports
Cars"></A>
<A  HREF="fast.htm"><IMG  SRC="fast.gif"  width=100  border=0  alt="Fast
Cars"></A>
<A HREF="racing.htm"><IMG SRC="racing.gif" width=100 border=0 alt="Racing
Cars"></A>
<BR><BR>
<IMG SRC="97viper.gif" width=250>
<BR><BR>

<!—We make use of a table to create two columns of text—>

<table width=500 border=0 cellpadding=5>
<tr>
<td> Welcome to <B>Pedal to the Metal</B>. Here you can find out about
any car that has been made at any time in history. Search by category or
manufacturer, year or model.</td>
<td> Each category conatins a fully interactive showroom where you can
view any car ever made in your choice of colour with any extras you desire.
Just sit back and enjoy the ride! </td>
<tr></table>
<p>  We hope you enjoyed our site.<BR>

<!—This is where visitors have the opportunity to email the Web site
owner directly —>

To make any comments, criticisms or otherwise, please contact the webmaster
at <A HREF="mailto:pedalmetal@hotmetal.co.uk">HotMetal</a><BR><BR>
</font color></p></center></BODY></HTML>
```

Conclusion

These examples were designed to be simple to follow and easy to replicate. Feel free to copy or borrow parts of them in your own creations. As you get more adventurous, you can use your Web browser to look at the HTML code of some of your favourite Web sites (most browsers give you this option. For example, in Internet Explorer 4, select Source from the View menu). This will help you learn new tricks, and provide "live" examples of how other people structure their Web pages to achieve a desired effect.

Chapter 8

Web Authoring Programs

In the previous chapter, we examined the basic structure of HTML, and the types of tags that new users are likely to enlist when creating their first Web site. As you will find from the resources listed at the end of the chapter, there is a lot more to HTML than the basic tags we covered.

Thankfully, users need no longer acquaint themselves with the ins and outs of every HTML tag before being in a position to create professional looking, creative and interesting Web sites. There is now a number of point-n-click, WYSIWYG ("what-you-see-is-what-you-get") Web authoring programs available.

These programs allow you to manipulate text and graphics within a Web document without ever worrying about the underlying HTML. Want to insert an image? Open the appropriate file menu, select the image you want and point your mouse to where you want it placed. Want to use a different size or style font? Simple. Highlight the text to be changed, and select the desired style from the menu. All the relevant options and functions are available via menu and toolbar options, and while you create and edit your Web page, it is displayed exactly as it should appear in a Web browser.

In this chapter, we will look at two of the most user-friendly Web authoring programs available and recommend a few others. While they are commercial programs (you have to pay for them if you want to use them), there are demonstration versions of each program available, so you can try before you buy.

PageMill (Windows & Macintosh)

PageMill is a Web authoring program from Adobe, a company famous for its desktop publishing programs. You can download a free, fully functional 15-day trial version of PageMill from the Adobe Web site at www.adobe.com/.

When you run PageMill for the first time, you will be presented with what looks like a fairly complex working environment. Don't worry – it is fairly intuitive, and you'll get the hang of it in no time. As mentioned earlier, inserting text and graphics is quite an easy task, similar to using a wordprocessor.

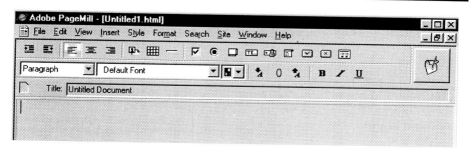

The Adobe PageMill interface looks a little complex,
but it is quite intuitive.

One of the first time saving tools that you should get to know is the Inspector Palette. The Inspector Palette is displayed when you press the F8 function key. Pressing F8 again hides the Palette.

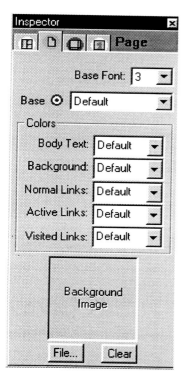

The Inspector Palette has four panels, each of which offer functions and shortcuts for different aspects of the Web creation process. The Palette displays the Page panel by default. The Page panel is used to set the basic parameters of how your Web document and the text that it contains will look when it is displayed in a Web browser. The others are the Frames, Forms and Object panels. They are used to control some of the more advances aspects of Web documents, and as such are beyond the scope of this introduction.

The options available in the Page panel are as follows:

Base Font – This is where you set the size of the font that you wish to use in your Web document (that is, how big or small the text appears on the user's screen)

Base – This menu provides options for creating either a simple Web document or one that uses Frames. Unless you have some experience in creating Web documents, you should keep the default setting.

Body Text – This menu allows users to specify what colour the text should appear in. The default setting is black. If you would like to use another colour, click on the pull down menu and click on

The Inspector Palette will soon become your friend, as it saves considerable editing time.

Custom. The Color dialogue box will appear providing you with a range of colours to select from. Click on the colour box that you prefer, then click on the OK button. If you have correctly selected a new colour, it will be displayed in the Body Text box.

Background – This menu allows you to set the background colour of your Web site. By default it is grey, however, you can change it via the Color dialogue box in the same way as you change the Body Text colour. Be sure to avoid choosing a background colour that conflicts with your selected body text colour, otherwise your Web document will be fairly difficult to read.

Normal, Active & Visited Links – These menus are used to change the colours used to indicate the presence of hyperlinks. The Normal setting selects the default colour used for text or images that contain a hyperlink. The Active setting selects the colour which hyperlinks turn to when they are clicked on. Finally, the Visited setting selects the colour used to indicate that the user has already followed a particular hyperlink.

Background Image – The final option is used to insert a background image – that is, an image that will appear behind the contents of your Web page. Many companies use their logo as a background image. Clicking on the File button displays the Open dialogue box, via which you select the graphic file you wish to use as the background image.

Your first Web document

Let's put some of what we have learnt so far into practice. Adobe PageMill works in one of two modes: edit & preview. The icon in the top right hand corner of the PageMill window indicates the current mode. In edit mode, the icon resembles a notepad and paper. In preview mode, it resembles a globe. You can switch between the two modes by clicking on the icon. When you wish to add, edit or modify the contents of your Web document, PageMill must be in edit mode. Once you have made your changes, you can see how your Web document will look when displayed by a Web browser by changing to preview mode.

For now, ensure that PageMill is in edit mode.

The standard for most Web documents is black text on a white background, with a font size between four or five. We will use green as the colour for hyperlinks (the default is light blue), and select red as the colour used for visited hyperlinks.

Click on the Base Font pull down menu in the Inspector Palette, and click on four. Next, click on the Background pull down menu, and select white from the available colours,. Do the same for the Normal and Visited menus, selecting green and red respectively. PageMill's window area that you use to insert text and graphics is called the "canvass".

It is now time to start inserting text and images into your document. Click inside the canvass window. A blinking cursor should appear, which indicates that it is ready for your keyboard input.

Enter the following text, pressing return at the end of each line:

This is my sample Web document
This line will be displayed in bold
This line will be displayed in italics
This line will be centred

Now, move your mouse pointer to the beginning of the first line, and mark the text by dragging the pointer over it. We will make this line the heading for the document. Headings are generally displayed using larger text characters. To change the sentence into a header, click on the Change Format pull-down toolbar menu (it displays the Paragraph format by default) and select Largest Heading.

The marked sentence will change to reflect its new status as a heading. Play around with the other Heading settings, to get an idea of the difference between the Smallest Heading and the Largest Heading settings.

Now lets move onto the next line. Mark the text in the same manner as you did the first line. This time, to turn the text into boldface text, click on the small B toolbar icon (towards the top left hand side of the toolbar). The marked text should now be displayed in bold.

Mark the next line and this time click on the italicised I icon (which is next to the bold icon). The text should now appear in italics.

Finally, highlight the last line of text and click on the Center Align Text icon (which is the middle of the last three active icons on the right side of the toolbar). The text should be moved to the centre of the document.

If you have trouble finding an icon, or if you are curious about what an icon does, move your mouse pointer over it and let it rest there for a second or two. A small text box will appear giving a brief description of the icon.

We will shortly look at the process of inserting hyperlinks and images into Web documents. But first let's take care of a few "administrative" matters.

When a user's Web browser displays your Web document, the document's title will be displayed at the top of the browser window. This serves two purposes. It can be used to give the user a ready summary of the contents of your document. Also, should the user "bookmark" the Web document, the title of the document will appear in the bookmark line, making it easier for the user to recall the nature of the bookmarked resource.

To give your document a title, click in the Title text box (which sits on top of the editing window). When you click in the Title box, it will change from grey to white and a cursor will appear, indicating that you can edit or insert a new title. Let's name our document "My Sample Web page".

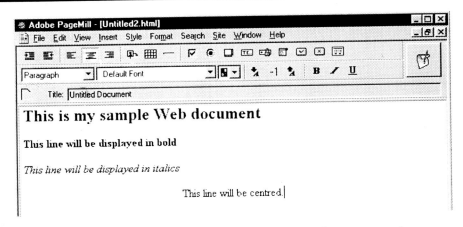

Your masterpiece-in-progress should look the same as the above PageMill document.

Finally, let's save a copy of our document. There are two ways to do this. First, you could click on the File menu, then select Save Page. Alternatively, you can use the ctrl-s hotkey. As it is the first time you are saving the document, the Save As dialogue box will appear, via which you can specify a filename for the document, and select where you wish to save it.

Most Web Servers (that is, computers which host Web sites) require that the main document (that is, the first Web page displayed to users when they connect to your Web site) be called index.html. You can call your secondary Web documents (that is, those to which the main index.html Web document contains links to) pretty well whatever you want. For the purposes of the current example, call this document index.html

Getting Heavy

As you can see from the above, creating the basic text of your Web document is a very simple task indeed. But what would a Web document be without hyperlinks and graphics?

Using graphics

As mentioned in an earlier chapter, the GIF and JPEG images are "native" to the Web – these are the default graphic formats supported by Web browsers. While Web browsers are able to display other image formats, they can only do so with the assistance of other programs (generally referred to as "plugins"). As you cannot assume that everyone who visits your Web site will have these plugins installed, it is generally a good idea to restrict yourself to using GIF and JPEG images.

Once you have the images that you want to use in either GIF or JPEG format, adding them to your Web documents is a relatively straightforward process. In this example, I will add a logo, which I've saved in GIF format, to our sample Web document.

The first step is to click our mouse pointer to roughly the point where we would like to insert the image. I've chosen the bottom of the document. The starting position isn't important, as we can move the image later on.

Next, click on the Insert Object toolbar button, or click on the Insert menu and select Object, then select Image from the sub-menu that appears. In either case, the Insert Object dialogue box will appear, via which you can select the image file that you wish to insert. Highlight the graphic file that you want to insert by clicking on it once, then click on the Open button.

The selected image will then be inserted into your Web document at the specified place. It will be displayed in the PageMill window, so that you can move it or otherwise manipulate it.

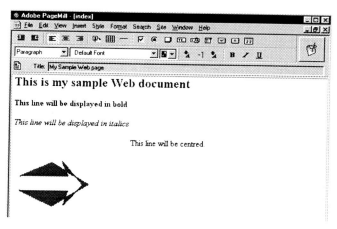

PageMill displays the inserted image so that you can manipulate it later on.

Now that the image is inserted, it looks a little out of place at the bottom, and would look better at the top left corner of the document. As mentioned, moving the image is not a problem. Click on the image once and, while holding your mouse button down, drag the image to the new position.

It looks a little silly having the image right next to the 1st line of text. To drop the heading down to the next line, position your cursor next to the start of the line of text (by clicking there) and press the Enter key. The heading should drop down to the next line. Much better! Now, let's move the image to the centre of the screen, by clicking on the Center Align Text icon.

To get a "preview" of how the Web document will look in a Web browser, turn PageMill into preview mode by clicking the icon in the top left hand corner of the window.

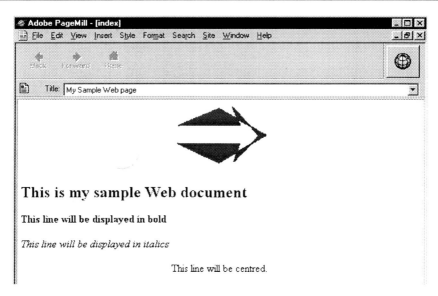

The finished product.

Inserting Hyperlinks

Finally, lets look at how PageMill deals with hyperlinks. We insert a hyperlink so that when the viewers of our sample Web document click on the logo, they will be taken to the Net.Works Web site (which is at www.net-works.co.uk).

First of all, put PageMill back into edit mode by clicking on the icon in the top left hand corner again. Next, click once on the image so that it is highlighted (a small box frame will appear around the image).

At the very bottom of the PageMill window is a text box titled Link To:. Click once in this box to turn it from grey to white, which indicates that it is ready to accept input. Then type "www.net-works.co.uk" (or whichever Web site you might want to refer visitors to) in the box, and then press Enter.

The text box will become grey again, but the URL remains in the box, indicating that we have been successful in placing the hyperlink. If the Inspector Palette is displayed, it will automatically swap to the Object Tab, so that you can make any desired changes to the image's settings. At the bottom of the Tab is the Border text box. The default value is 0, which means that the image will not be surrounded by a border to indicate the presence of a hyperlink. If you like, set the value to 1, to display a green border as a visual reminder of the presence of a hyperlink (remember, we selected green as the colour to be used to display hyperlinks).

Now, we used the example of inserting a hyperlink in an image. We could have just as easily inserted a hyperlink in a word, or a section of text. To do this, you need only mark the word or section of text, then click in the Link To: field and enter the details of the linked Web site in the same manner shown above.

Multiple page Web sites

Of course, hyperlinks aren't limited to links to other Web sites. Your Web site might consist of many pages of text. For example, you might use your main Web page (index.html) to list a series of links to other areas of your Web site (which are comprised of individual documents).

> **Web design isn't true WYSIWYG. The language HTML is designed as a "structural markup language"; that is, its focus is on the structure of documents, not their layout. As such, it does not give the author absolute control over the final product, and there are a number of issues that may affect the way in which your Web pages are displayed on the visitor's computer screen. Therefore you should always test your creations using different browsers and (preferably) different computers.**

Take the case of a car dealership. Its Web site might consist of five Web documents. The main Web page (index.html) contains the logo of the car dealership, a brief discussion of the business, and then links to four separate Web documents, each of which contains a photo of a car for sale and a brief description.

Now, in the main Web document (index.html), the names of each model advertised on the secondary Web documents would contain hyperlinks, so that visitors could move to those pages by clicking on the name of the model. Those hyperlinks would be inserted in the same manner discussed above, but instead of referring to the URL of a Web site, the name of the Web document would be inserted in the Link To: box (e.g. model1.html, model2.html etc.).

Great for Beginners

PageMill is a very easy to use program, and quite suitable for beginners. One of its best features is that it allows users to take a look at the underlying HTML of their Web documents and, if they want, to manually edit the HTML. This is not particularly useful for new users, but once you get the hang of HTML, you might find that is easier to manually add to or modify HTML documents when you only want to make minor corrections or to experiment.

For further information about PageMill, visit the Adobe PageMill technical support site at www.adobe.com/supportservice/custsupport/TECHGUIDE/PMILL/main.html. The trial version of PageMill comes with an interactive tutorial, which will guide you through PageMill's major features and options.

FrontPage (Windows & Macintosh)

Another popular Web authoring program is Microsoft's Frontpage. It, too, is a simple, WYSIWYG Web authoring program. Its look and feel is much like a desktop publishing or wordprocessing package, yet it allows users to create visually impressive Web sites without any knowledge of HTML.

You can download a trial version of Microsoft FrontPage from www.microsoft.com/frontpage/. There you will also find extensive online help, Web authoring tips and tricks, and links to information about products and services offered by other companies for use with FrontPage.

Using FrontPage

In the earlier PageMill example, we looked at how to create a basic Web page from scratch. In this example, we will create a basic but effective business Web page using one of FrontPage's many "wizards".

FrontPage has a number of template Web pages available to users, ranging from simple, one-page personal Web sites, though to more complex corporate-style Web sites. Using these template "wizards" is pretty much a process of filling-in-the-blanks, as we shall shortly see.

When you run FrontPage for the first time, it will check to see whether your PC is configured for Internet access and, if so, record your Internet address details (this makes uploading your Web page much easier).

Once it has completed this task, it will then present you with the New FrontPage Web dialogue box.

Select the Corporate Presence Wizard.

You will need to specify a location that FrontPage will used to store your Web files. Click in the Change button and FrontPage will show you the default location. This should be suitable for most readers. Click on the OK button to accept the default location.

Next, choose a name for your Web site and type it in the box

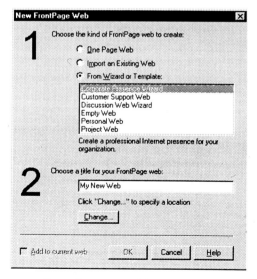

FrontPage provides users with a handy collection of Web page wizards.

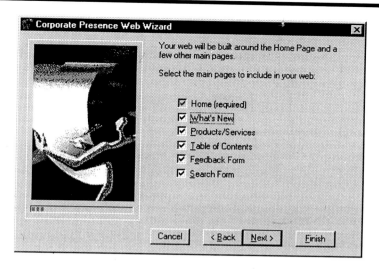

The Wizard provides you with a shopping list of different Web components

provided. Once you have done this, click on the OK button to begin creating your new Web site.

The Corporate Presence Web Wizard dialogue box will appear. The wizard will guide you though the process of creating your first page. Click Next to continue.

The next screen will offer you a collection of different Web components that you can include in your Web site, including a feedback form and a table of contents. Select the components that you would like, then click Next to continue.

The next step is to select what information you wish to appear on your main Web site screen. At the very least, you should select Contact Information from the wizard options.

Before you can use FrontPage, you must have Microsoft's Personal Web Server software installed on your computer. This will normally be installed as part of the FrontPage software. If, for some reason, it isn't, you can download a copy from www.microsoft.com/ie/download/. You will need to install the Personal Web Server software before you can use FrontPage.

The Corporate Presence Web Wizard will then step you through each additional component of your Web site, offering you further choices of information and features that you can include on your site. It will even allow you to select a "theme" for your Web page, giving it a professional look.

Once the Wizard has guided you through the process of selecting the features of your new Web site, it will then automatically create one or more Web files which, together, constitute your new Web page. So far, so good!

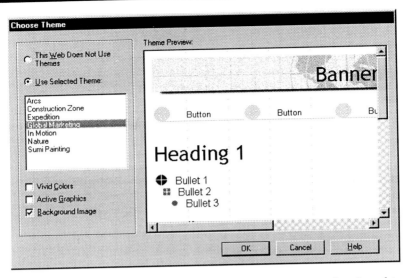

Choose a theme for your Web site to give it a more professional touch.

Task List

Once the Wizard has completed automatically generating your Web site, FrontPage will display a list of tasks that you will need to complete to finalise your Web site. These basically include providing the text that will appear on the various sections of your Web site.

To perform a task, double click on it. The Tasks Details dialogue window will appear, giving you general details of the task. Click on the Do Task button to get going.

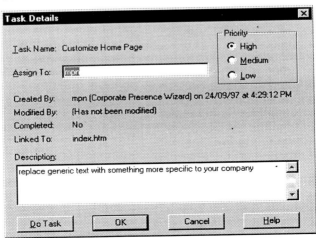

The task manager lets you know what needs to be done with your Web site.

The first task is to "customise" your home page (the main Web site page). This is basically a matter of filling in the dotted lines, as FrontPage has created all the necessary graphics and authored the corresponding HTML.

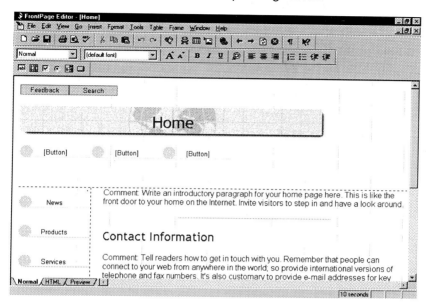

FrontPage does all the hard work – it is now all a matter of point-click-n-type.

Once you have edited the various components of your Web site, all you need to do is upload the files to your Web site!

Customising your site

While FrontPage's templates are a great service for the uninitiated, many users will want to use them as a guide only, adding their own graphics and content areas as they go. FrontPage certainly accommodates this.

It is recommended that those new to Web authoring use a wizard to create their basic Web site (even if it does not do everything that you want). Then you can go back and use FrontPage's menu and toolbar functions to edit, manipulate and insert new content and graphics. As with PageMill, FrontPage is very intuitive in this regard.

If you need further assistance creating or manipulating your basic Web site, FrontPage has extensive help menus, and the FrontPage Web site (www.microsoft.com/frontpage/) offers a range of how-to style tutorials and articles to point you in the right direction.

Worth Trying

There are a number of other WYSIWYG and semi-WYSIWYG Web authoring programs available. Here are some more to investigate:

HotMetal Pro (Windows)

One of the veterans in the Web authoring arena.

HotMetal, by SoftQuad (www.softquad.com) is one of the "grandfathers" of Web authoring, having been available to Web developers for several years before products such as FrontPage. It benefits from this maturity, offering users an intuitive authoring environment that can be customised to user preferences.

In addition to a flexible editing environment, HotMetal Pro also offers users a range of "wizards" to guide them through everything from basic Web site authoring to selecting and implementing a common Web site theme and layout. In addition, HotMetal Pro contains several image creation/manipulation programs that can come in handy when creating your own images, or manipulating existing ones.

HotMetal Pro is excellent for users who can see themselves progressing from a beginner to an intermediate web designer. All of Net-works web sites (four) are created using HotMetal Pro.

DreamWeaver
(Windows & Macintosh)

DreamWeaver is a relatively recent offering from Macromedia (www.macromedia.com), better known for their Shockwave Web multimedia tools. Although the package is aimed at the professional Web developer, its interface is reasonably intuitive, and can be picked up quite quickly by computer literate users.

If you expect to invest a lot of time and effort creating, maintaining and updating your Web site, your investment in getting to know this program will be repaid in full once your skills are developed to such a level that you can take full advantage of all the program has to offer.

Symantec Visual Page
(Windows & Macintosh)

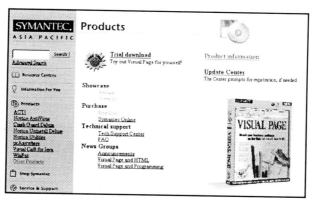

Symantec's Visual Page is aimed at the novice user.

Symantec (www.symantec.com) are better known for their programming utilities, disk repair and anti-virus software. However, they have produced a simple Web authoring program that is quite beginner-friendly. Although (at the time of writing) it lacks support for some of the more advanced aspects of Web authoring, what it does support it supports well. New users will have little trouble familiarising themselves with the user interface, and the built-in tutorial should answer any questions

Conclusion

These programs are only some of a number of helpful, beginner-friendly Web authoring programs. Each tends to have its own strengths and weaknesses, and at the end of the day the "best" program really is a subjective decision. Be sure to download and try a few different programs, to see which one best suits your needs.

Chapter 9

Publishing Your Web Site

O nce you have designed your Web site using your favourite Web authoring program and tested it by viewing the files on your PC using your Web browser(s), you are ready to upload your Web site. As a general rule, once you have uploaded your Web site files to your Internet account, the site becomes publicly viewable — that is, anyone can connect to your Web site and view it, as long as they know its URL.

What you need

In order to upload your Web site, you need the following:

✔ Details of the specific Internet host (or Web Server) and directory to which you must upload your files (your Internet service provider should be able to provide you with the necessary information - see below), and

✔ An ftp ("file transfer protocol") program to move files to and from your Web site.

Web Server

Most Internet Service Providers (ISPs) now provide their users with space on their Web Servers in which they can host their own Web sites. As a general rule, you must connect to your ISP's Web Server, provide your userid and password to log in, and then upload your Web files to a specific directory.

Your ISP should provide you with information on how to do this. You will need to know:

✔ The Internet address of the Web Server (or other host machine) that you should connect to;

✔ The procedure required to log on;

✔ Whether you need to create a special directory to store your Web files (and, if so, what you should call that directory); and

✔ Whether you need to name your Web site files with specific names or file extensions.

Several ISPs now make the process of configuring your Internet account for Web hosting a breeze. They provide special "wizards" on their Web sites which — once you have supplied your userid and password — will create any special directory or files needed on the Web Server to get your Web site up and running. It is then a simple matter of uploading your files to the Web Server.

If your ISP does not allow users to store their Web pages on their Web Server, there are a number of free and commercial Web hosting services available that you can use to publish your Web site. See the list of resources at the end of this chapter.

File transfer program

FTP is the Internet protocol that regulates how files are transferred across the Internet (in fact, "FTP" stands for "file transfer protocol"). There are quite a number of FTP programs available. Two of the most popular ones for Windows users are WS_FTP and CuteFTP. Two of the more popular Mac FTP programs are Anarchie and Fetch. You will find details of where you can download these programs at the end of the chapter.

The example in this chapter uses WS_FTP. However, the basic elements of FTP programs are fairly standard, and the concepts that you learn in this example will be applicable to any FTP program that you decide to use.

❑ Start WS_FTP by clicking on the icon created by the program when you installed it. WS_FTP will run, displaying the default Session Profile window.

❑ If you have the details provided to you by your ISP handy, you should create a Session Profile for your Web site. This will save you from having to re-enter the details each time you want to upload files to your Web site. Click on the New button near the top of the Session Profile window; the program will display a blank Session Profile window.

❑ Enter the details required. These include:

❑ Profile Name. Give your profile a name for future reference, such as My Web Site. Next time you run WS_FTP, you will be able to select it from the list of available profiles.

❑ Host Name. Enter the Internet address of your ISP's Web server.

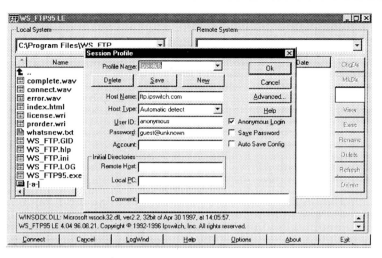

The WS_FTP opening screen.

❑   Host Type. Leave this set to Automatic Detect.

❑   User ID. Your userid (or the userid that your ISP instructs you to use)

❑   Password. Your password (or the password that your ISP instructs you to use)

❑   Account. Leave blank unless instructed to use a specific account by your ISP

The Initial Directories section in the Startup Tab is available for your convenience. If you store your Web site files in a specific directory on your hard disk (your computer is referred to as the "Local PC") or if you are required to upload your Web site files to a specific directory on your ISP's Web server ("Remote Host"), enter the details and WS_FTP will use these each time you start it.

Toggle the Auto-Save Config and Save Password options so that they are ticked. Do not, however, toggle the Anonymous Password option, as this causes WS_FTP to supply a generic password to the Web Server, rather than your password, which will generate an error message.

Connecting to the Web server

Once you have entered the details, and checked that there are no typographical errors, click on the OK button. WS_FTP will then attempt to connect to the Web Server, and log in using the userid and password specified. If all goes well, it will log you in and display the contents of your Internet account.

The screen is divided in two. In the left window (titled "Local System"), the contents of the default directory of your hard disk (generally the directory that

WS_FTP is installed in, unless you specified otherwise in the Initial Directories option). In the right window (titled "Remote System"), the contents of your Internet account are displayed.

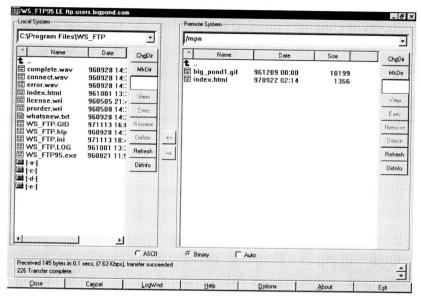

WS_FTP allows you to view the contents of both your hard disk and your Internet account.

Uploading files

Open the directory that contains your Web site files in the left (Local System) window. You can move from one directory on your hard disk to another by clicking on the relevant drive volume identifier (c: for most hard disks) and then selecting the relevant directory from the list displayed).

Once you have opened the relevant directory in the Local System window, highlight a file that you wish to transfer by clicking on it once. Then click on the arrow pointing to the Remote System window (located on the pane between the two windows). WS_FTP will then copy the file to your Internet account (the original will still be on your computer). Unless it is a sizeable file (such as a graphic), uploading should occur in a matter of seconds!

Downloading files (that is, copying them from your Internet account to your computer) is achieved in the same way — highlight the name of a file displayed in the Remote System window, then click on the arrow pointing to the Local System window.

You can upload multiple files at a time by holding the control (ctrl) key down as you click on them.

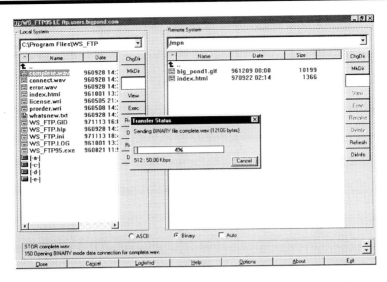

***WS_FTP displays a status bar that will keep you informed of the progress
of your file transfers.***

A word of warning about filenames. Most Web Servers use the Unix operating
system. Unix is very case sensitive, unlike Windows and Macs. You must ensure that
your filenames use upper and lower case in a uniform fashion. To a Unix Web
Server, index.html and Index.html are completely different files.

If your Web documents refer to a file, such as page2.html, then it must be
named page2.html, not page2.HTML or Page2.html. This is one of the most common causes of problems when publishing Web documents. It is always a good idea
to adopt a uniform method of naming files (e.g. lower case only) and stick to it, so as
to avoid this problem.

Testing your site

Even though you tested your Web site by viewing the files on your hard disk with a
Web browser, it is a good idea to test your Web site after you have uploaded it
before you start publicising it.

You should check for a number of things:

- How quickly your Web site loads (there will be a marked difference between
  the time it takes to load from your hard disk, and the time required for the text
  and graphics to be downloaded and displayed from your Internet site).
- Obvious errors (such as typographical errors)
- Missing or corrupt graphic images.

You should preview your Web site using at least both Internet Explorer and Netscape Navigator (these are the two most popular Web browsers). Although they perform the same task (that is, display Web documents), they have certain differences in terms of how your files can actually appear. Although the differences are fairly minor, they can have a major effect on what your visitors see.

A common problem is "missing" graphic images. Sometimes it's a question of using the "Shift" key: as mentioned earlier, most Web Servers are case-sensitive, and have no way of knowing that "logo.jpg" is the same as "Logo.jpg". Make sure that your pages contain the exact names that your files will have. Also, you should make sure that your graphic and image files are in the same directory as the rest of your Web files. This is not a strict rule, as it's possible to organise files of different types into specific directories, but beginners usually find it easier to troubleshoot their sites when all the files are in the same place.

As you get more confident with Web designing, and develop more complex sites, you will find that it is often convenient to separate files into different directories (e.g. images in one directory, major Web documents in another, with different directories for each area of your Web site etc.). But for now, work on using a flat directory structure, and lump all your files in the same directory.

Before you give your Web site a test viewing, make sure that you "flush" your Web browser's cache. Web browsers store copies of recently viewed Web sites in a special cache directory on your hard disk. If you revisit a Web site whose files are stored in the cache, your Web browser will load the files from the cache (as this is faster than downloading the files again). When you view your Web site online, your Web browser might try to load the (now obsolete) files from its cache. If you do not want to flush the cache, you can achieve the same end by clicking on your Web browser's Reload button.

HTML validation services

As a final measure before you commence publicising your Web site, you might like to take advantage of one of the many HTML validation services.

These services have special programs that will visit your Web site and scan your Web documents for errors in your HTML. If they find any errors or problems that might give rise to difficulties when viewed with a specific browser, they will report back to you (usually through email) with a summary of the problem, and often a hint for how to remedy it. Some validation services will even pick up on your spelling mistakes (beware of US sites that will only offer US-English spelling corrections, however)!

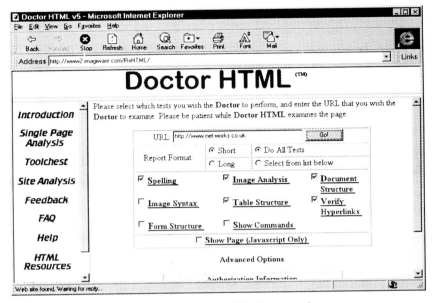

The Doctor HTML validation service

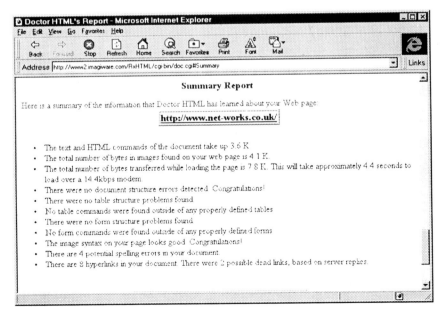

Doctor HTML provides detailed results that will help you pinpoint potential problems.

Some of the better HTML validators are:

- **WebTechs** - www.webtechs.com/html-val-svc
- **HTML Chek** - uts.cc.utexas.edu/~churchh/htmlchek.html
- **Dr HTML** - www2.imagiware.com/RxHTML/
- **Bobby** - www.cast.org/bobby/
- or for a **list** of checkers, go to www.flfsoft.com/html/html_validators.html

These services are really for "peace of mind" than anything – modern Web authoring programs should already check for "compliant" code. But, it is better to be safe than sorry!

Resources

Free Web Hosting services

Geocities – www.geocities.com
Angelfire Communications - www.angelfire.com
HomeStead - www.homestead.com
Tripod - www.tripod.com

FTP programs

Arnarchie - http://www.share.com/peterlewis/
Fetch - http://www.dartmouth.edu/pages/softdev/fetch.html
CuteFTP - http://www.cuteftp.com/
WS_FTP - http://www.ipswitch.com/Products/WS_FTP/index.html

Chapter 10

Bandwidth Constraints

If there is one word that you are guaranteed to hear about both as an Internet user and as a Web designer, it's bandwidth. The technical definition of bandwidth is: the maximum amount of data (text and images) that can be sent through a communications path in a given time (usually measured in megabytes per second, or Mbps). Most users conceptualise bandwidth in terms of pipes — the wider the pipe (that is, the higher its bandwidth) the more data that can flow through it at once.

Bandwidth is a very important – and perplexing — issue, especially from a Web designer's perspective.

As discussed in earlier chapters, if you don't grab your visitors' attention within 15 to 30 seconds of their arrival at your site, you run the risk that they will leave in search of more interesting fare. If your site is so complex, or its files so large, that it chokes the "pipe", it will take a long time to load, increasing the chances that visitors will abandon your site. But then, if you don't have anything interesting or visually stimulating to offer, the users are just as likely to disappear.

When it comes to online content, "interesting" etc. usually equates to "bandwidth-intensive". Balancing interesting and visually stimulating against bandwidth limitations can be a real dilemma. In this chapter, we will look at some strategies that you can adopt.

Some mathematics

While there are now some exciting technologies that allow high-speed Internet access at an affordable price (such as 56K modems, cable modems and ISDN), many Internet users access the Internet using older, slower technologies.

As such, it would be fair to assume that the average download speed achievable by your visitors is 3Kbps (that is, they can download three Kilobytes of data per second, or 0.003 Megabytes per second). If you were to create a Web site logo that is, say, 20Kb in size (which is quite small compared to some graphics in use on Web sites today), it would take roughly 7 seconds for that graphic to be downloaded and displayed on the user's screen (20/3 = 6.66).

Now, let's say that your Web site contained your logo, a nifty animated email icon, and four buttons used as hyperlinks to other areas of your Web site. We'll say for the sake of our calculations that the buttons were each 10kb in size, and that the animated email icon was slightly larger at 15kb. In total, your opening page (which some might say is quite Spartan, graphic-wise) would contain 75Kb of graphics. This would take the average user 25 seconds to download, and that is not including any text that your Web page might also contain (although the text will download quite quickly, unless you have literally pages and pages of text in the single Web document). As you can see, even a modest number of graphics cuts it pretty close to the 30-second rule.

Bandwidth tricks

Unless your Web site offers content that is so compelling that users will want to wait around for the graphics to download, you will maximise your chances that visitors will stick around and perhaps explore your Web site if you minimise your use of graphics.

This does not mean that you have to forsake colour and multimedia on your Web site. But it does mean that you have to work a little smarter. Here are some tricks for you to try:

Offer visitors "high bandwidth" and "low bandwidth" alternatives

It does not require too much effort to create "mirror" copies of your Web site. One version can use all the graphics and multimedia that you want to use; the other one should use minimal graphics for those who are in a hurry or who don't want to wait around for all your graphics to download.

Prefer the JPEG file format (.jpg) to GIF files (.gif) when saving custom-made graphics.

Images saved in JPEG format are, generally speaking, smaller files, as the format has better data compression. However, it is not always a simple matter of saving all your images as JPEGs, as the use of either format will affect image quality. Therefore, you must strive to obtain the best quality:size ratio. This will involve a bit of experimenting at first, until you get the hang of it.

Use a graphics manipulation program to compress image files

Either by saving them with greater compression or by converting them from one graphic format to another, such as from GIF to JPEG. There are a number of free or shareware graphics manipulation programs available for download.

Reuse graphics on your Web site where possible.

Once a user's Web browser has downloaded a graphic image, it will generally be stored in a local "cache" on the user's hard disk. If they revisit your Web site or if they access another area of your Web site that uses the same graphic, the Web browser will use the copy of the image stored in the cache, rather than re-download it. This speeds up the display of graphics considerably.

Avoid cool tricks. Many Web authoring programs have 'wizards' that automate the process of adding "cool" effects to your Web site, including flashing and scrolling text. Unless there is a very specific reason for using these types of effects, you should avoid them completely. They might look interesting the first time you see them, but once you see it for the second and third time, they can get a little tedious! But, perhaps more to the point, they use up a lot of valuable bandwidth.

Use a reduced colour palette.

Most graphics programs work with colour palettes, which determine the amount of colours that can be used within a specific image. GIF images, for example, generally work with an 8-bit palette, with the result that up to 256 colours can be used within a single image. Most Web graphics, however, don't use anywhere near as many colours. Few graphics use more than four or eight colours. By reducing the number of colours available in the palette used to create an image, you can achieve considerable savings in file sizes. For example, by using a 6-bit palette, you will still have access to 64 colours, but you will reduce your file sizes by around 25 percent.

If you must use a background image, use a very small image.

If the background image is used primarily to create a custom background colour, create only very small images (for example, 4 x 72 pixels). The Web browser will "tile" the image (that is, repeat it over and over again, filling the screen background). Also, there is no need to "interlace" background images, as this will add unnecessarily to the file's size. This is a handy trick for displaying larger images, but it is completely wasted on small, background images.

Unless you have a specific need for a custom background image, you should use the `<BODY BGCOLOR="xxxxxx">` HTML tag (see Chapter 6) to set the background colour, where "xxxxxx" is one of the standard colour names in HTML.

Save your images in low resolution.

The lower you set your image resolution, the smaller the resulting file will be. Unless you have a compelling need to publish images in high resolution (for example, if you are selling art online), you should not save your images in anything higher than 72dpi resolution.

Conclusion

Once you have "tweaked" your graphics and used as many bandwidth-conserving tricks as you can, ask a few friends to connect to your Web site and view it. Have them record the time it takes for the pages to load and compare the results.

Resources

The Bandwidth Conservation Society - www.infohiway.com/faster/index.html

JPEG Frequently Asked Question (FAQ) File - www.cis.ohio-state.edu/hypertext/faq/usenet/jpeg-faq/top.html

HTML for the World Wide Web —Visual QuickStart Guide (Chapter 3 — Images) - www.peachpit.com/peachpit/features/htmlvqs/htmlvqsfeature.html

Chapter 11

Promoting Your Web Site

It used to be that the simple act of publishing a Web site effectively guaranteed your site an audience. In the earlier years, there were few Web sites around, and those that did exist were fairly dry affairs used for scientific data dissemination.

That was then. This is now. Users are overwhelmed by choice, and competition for "eyeballs" is fierce. If you want to get people to visit your site, you have to work pretty hard at it.

The eyes have it

When the Web first began, users kept written lists of their favourite sites, or memorised the addresses of the ones that they used regularly. Today, maintaining a list of favourite sites by hand would be a full-time job in itself. Memorising them is out of the question.

Search engines were created to solve these problems. Search engines, such as Yahoo! (www.yahoo.com) and Alta Vista (http://www.altavista.digital.com/), are essentially massive indexes of known Web sites. Web robots scan the Internet all day every day for new Web sites. As new sites are found, their contents are indexed and the details stored in the Search engines' databases. Users can locate Web sites of interest by performing key word searches of the databases.

You probably gathered from all of this that search engines play an integral role in the site-promotion process. In fact, unless you have unlimited funds to promote your Web site using the more traditional advertising, listings with search engines will mean the difference between anonymity and celebrity!

Spreading the word

Registering your Web site with search engines is a relatively painless process. Basically, you visit one or more search engines and follow the prompts through the submission process. Most of the major Web sites have an Add URL button or link on their home page. "URL" stands for "uniform resource locator" — that is, the address of a Web site (the string of characters that begins with "http://").

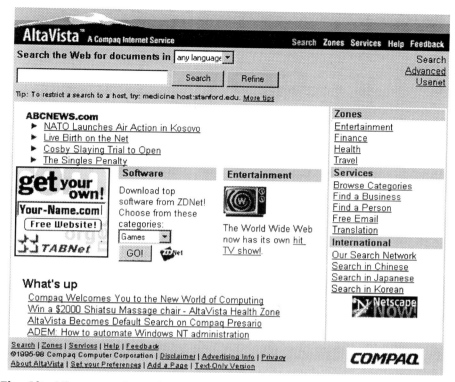

The Alta Vista search engine allows users to add Web sites to its directory through a link at the bottom of the home page (while you are here, note the option to see text-only and to set your own preferences for this site).

The search engines themselves generally use one of two methods for accepting additions to their databases.

The first method is to prompt you to specify the URL, or address of the Web site to be added to the database. Once provided, the search engine's Web robot handles the rest, visiting the Web site, indexing its contents and adding it to the search engine. Alta Vista is an example of a search engine that adopts this method.

Other search engines expect the user to do most of the "leg work", requiring that they submit all the necessary information about their Web site (such as who owns/maintains it, what type or category of information it contains) plus a short summary that tells potential visitors what the site contains. Yahoo! is one of several search engines that use this method.

> A small number of sites regularly submit a large number of pages to the AltaVista index in the hope of showing very frequently on our result pages. The usual technique is to submit pages with numerous keywords, or with keywords unrelated to the real content of the pages. Some people submit pages that present our spider with content that differs from what browsers will see. We strongly discourage the use of these techniques.
>
> AltaVista is an index, not a promotional tool. Attempts to fill it with promotional material lower the value of the index for everyone. Left unchecked, this behavior would make Web indexes worthless. We will disallow URL submissions from those who spam the index. In extreme cases, we will exclude all their pages from the index.

No SPAM Please!

```
http://                                          [ Submit URL ]
```

Our Network | Add/Remove URL | Feedback
Help | Advertising Info | About AltaVista

The Alta Vista URL submission page

Directories

Web directories play much the same role as search engines. Most Web directories maintain current listings of sites related to one or more topics. The majority of Web directories are "single topic": they list sites related to a single topic. Some of the more advanced directories offer limited search functions as well.

Web directories are an excellent place to list your Web site, as you can be sure that the individuals who use such services are looking for the information or products on offer at yours. For a list of available Web directories, check out the Resources section at the end of this chapter.

The 'Search Engine' Yahoo is actually a huge directory which is searchable. When you want to submit your URL to Yahoo you will need to locate which category of the directory your site should be in before you complete the on-line form.

To learn more about search engines, directories and meta-search-engines see *Find What You Want on the Internet*, also by Net.Works - details on page 109.

The Link Monster directory at www.linkmonster.com

Submission services

It really pays to invest some time registering your Web site with search engines and directories, and otherwise promoting your Web site. But what if you don't have the time? Working from search engine to search engine registering your Web site can certainly be tedious. Thankfully, there is a better way. A number of Web sites now offer automated promotion services. You supply the details of your Web site, and they will automatically submit its details to various search engines and directories.

Services of this nature can be a real blessing, especially if you want to get the word out about your Web site quickly. However, there are a few catches. The automated submission sites are generally free. But the sites are usually operated by professional Web marketing companies, who use the "free" services as a marketing tool for their other services. Some of the sites are little more than an advertisement for the pay-per-use services, but these tend to be in the minority.

Other services may submit your site to only a limited number of search engines. For example, Submit It! will register your Web site with 16 popular search engines for free, but also offers fee-based services that will register your Web site with up to 400 search engines, directories and other promotion vehicles.

But, even though they only submit your site to a limited number of search engines, you cannot complain about the cost — besides, there's nothing stopping you from using several different free promotion services!

The Submit IT promotion Web site at www.submit-it.com is an excellent resource for promoting your Web site.

Once you have registered your web site with a variety of search engines, directories, and other promotional web sites, it makes sense to review how your listings are working. You can do this using the services offered by PositionAgent, at http:// www.positionagent.com/ or RankThis! at http://www.rankthis.com/

Meta tags

Before you launch into promoting your Web site, here is a neat "trick" that you can use to help with the promotion process.

Most search engines and directories etc. support the use of meta tags. Meta tags operate as a kind of helpful hint for search engines and other online catalogues and directories. The tags are essentially a collection of keywords that describe your Web site and the contents and resources that it offers. Search engines can use them as guides when determining how to properly index and categorise your Web site. The most popular meta tags are the description and keyword tags.

The @Submit promotion service at www.uswebsites.com/submit/ will promote your Web site for free.

The content of the description meta tag is displayed by meta tag-enabled search engines when listing your site in the user's search results.

The contents of the keyword meta tag are used by search engines as part of their categorising process. Instead of sifting through the text of your Web site trying to pick appropriate key words, meta tag-enabled search engines will index your Web site according to the key words you supply.

Use as many keywords as you think appropriate, each separated by a comma (","). Try to keep them down to between 150 to 200 characters (including spaces). Most search engines will ignore repetitive key words. When selecting your key words, make sure that you are describing your Web site, not your company. People will be searching for information or products of interest. They will be a little disappointed if, after searching for information and being pointed to your Web site, it does not offer the information promised. For example, if your company offers computer training in popular Windows programs such as Excel, PowerPoint, Word and Access, but your Web site only contains information on how to make better use of 'Excel', then be sure to limit your meta-tags to Excel, and not use them to describe the other services your company may offer but which do not appear on the Web site.

Meta tags should appear between the `<HEAD>` tags in your Web documents. They are used as follows:

```
<HEAD>
 <TITLE>Title</TITLE>
 <META Name="description" Content="Write your description here">
 <META Name="keywords" Content="Write, your, keywords, here">
 </HEAD>
```

If you're not sure which meta tags to use for your site, don't worry, there are programs that will prepare them for you. See the resources listed at the end of the chapter for pointers.

Banners

Another form of effective promotion is through the use of banners. We discussed in Chapter 4 how you could use banners to advertise the contents of your site to visitors once they were there. But you can also use banners to attract visitors from other Web sites.

There are generally three ways to achieve this. The first is to pay for advertising space on popular Web sites, such as Yahoo! or C|Net (www.cnet.com). For most Web site owners, this is far too expensive.

The second alternative is to enter into a banner exchange agreement with one or more friendly Web site owners. Basically, you agree to include their banner (or banners) on your Web site if they agree to include your banners on theirs. This can be especially useful if you can partner with Web sites that contain information or services similar to yours. For example, if yours is a hobby Web site discussing scuba diving, you might swap banners with other scuba enthusiasts' sites. Similarly, if your Web site sells fitness equipment, you might swap banners with a fitness-related Web site.

The third alternative is basically a more organised version of the second. There now exist a number of professionally organised "banner exchange" services. Although each has subtle variations, they basically work like this: you register your Web site with the co-ordinating Web site and supply a copy of your banner (or banners). Yours are then added to a database of available banners. In return for

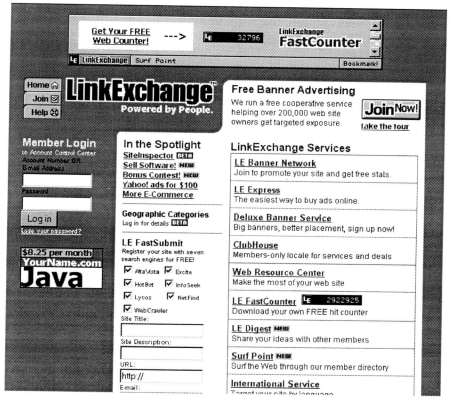

Internet Link Exchange (www.linkexchange.com)
offers free banner placements.

access to this service — which is free — you must agree to display the banners of other banner exchange members on your Web site. Often you are given some special HTML code to insert on your Web pages to do this.

Once you modify your Web site with the special HTML code, a banner from one of the banner exchange members will be displayed on your Web site. But instead of displaying the one, static banner, a new banner is displayed each time a visitor comes to your Web site. Each time a banner is displayed on your Web site, you receive a "credit". The banner exchange's computers track these credits and the number of credits earned by your Web site dictates both the number of sites that display your own banners and the frequency at which they are displayed. It sounds complex, but it is both easy to implement and beneficial to all participants.

There are quite a number of different banner exchange programs. You'll find a few pointers to some of them in the resources section overleaf.

Resources

Web search engines

For an exhaustive list of Web Search engines, check Yahoo!'s listing at:
> http://www.yahoo.com/Computers_and_Internet/Internet/
> World_Wide_Web/Searching_the_Web/Search_Engines/

Web directories

For an exhaustive list of Web directories, check Yahoo!'s listing at:
> http://www.yahoo.com/Computers_and_Internet/Internet/
> World_Wide_Web/Searching_the_Web/Web_Directories/

Promotion services

The following Web sites offer free submission services:
> **The Submitter:** http://www.thewebsubmitter.com/
> **Submit It:** http://www.submit-it.com/
> **@Submit:** http://www.uswebsites.com/submit/
> **ROBO-Submit:** http://www.inetwebs.com/ROBO/
> **Add Me:** http://www.addme.com/
> **Register-It:** http://www.register-it.com/

For a more comprehensive list, visit Yahoo!'s list at:
> http://www.yahoo.com/Business_and_Economy/Companies/
> Internet_Services/Web_Services/Promotion

Promotion software

Some of these programs are free, others are pay-per-use. All will save you time and hassle.
> **Web Site Promoter Engine:** http://www.flinet.com/~emeyers/wspe.shtml
> **The Art of Business Web site Promotion:** http://deadlock.com/promote/

Meta tag generators

> **Meta Tag Builder:** http://vancouver-webpages.com/VVbot/mk-metas.html
> **Meta Tag Generator:** http://www.websitepromote.com/resources/meta/

Banner exchange

> **Banner Swap:** http://www.bannerswap.com/
> **Better Deals:** http://www.betterdeals.com/
> **Internet Link Exchange:** http://www.linkexchange.com/
> **Smart Clicks:** http://www.smartclicks.com/

Chapter 12

The Good, The Bad, and The Ugly

In previous chapters we have looked at the "theory" behind what works on the Web and what doesn't. In later chapters, we looked at how you could put some of that theory into practice when creating your own Web sites. In this chapter we provide some solid examples of the theory in practice, but critiquing a number of high profile — and some less well known — Web sites.

Remember, however, that as with most aesthetic issues, what "works" and what doesn't is often purely a matter of personal taste. That said, this chapter should give you an idea of how to view your Web site masterpiece through the eyes of others.

The Electric Library (www.elibrary.com)

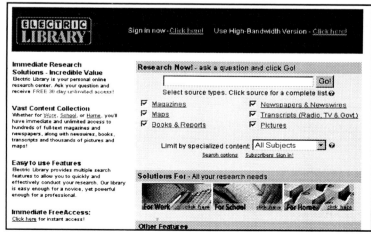

The Electronic Library is an excellent resource for Internet users.

Overall the site demonstrates good planning. The left side of the screen is used for a short summary of what the site offers, and then a series of navigational aids (which use plain-text hyperlinks rather than icons to save bandwidth). The reader is immediately presented with a search box, so that those familiar with the site (or search facilities in general) can immediately use the site productively.

The main home page has obviously been designed with speed in mind. The logo in the top left-hand corner is quite compact, both in terms of space occupied on the screen and in file size (less than 2Kb). Interestingly, the site's designer has incorporated a banner advertisement directly into the logo (presumably this was also done to save bandwidth). Once you navigate into the site, the logo becomes a separate graphic, and a background graphic is used to help "brand" the site. Both the new logo and background are re-used throughout the site, so users need only download them once.

The site is available in two versions: low and high bandwidth. Users are presented with the low bandwidth site by default, but can choose to view the high bandwidth site (which makes more use of graphics, especially for navigational icons).

The Electronic Library Web site offers a welcome section introducing you to the site and informing you what they are trying to say and what they are about. This could have been a bit more of an eye catcher — perhaps displayed in a panel or a different colour.

Navigational options are well planned and the icons and general layout of the site communicate to visitors quite clearly what their options are. The site is educational, informative and well presented — an excellent resource.

Cybertown (www.cybertown.com)

Cybertown is a fairly slick Web site, with great graphics that, while on the large side (the main graphic at the top of the page is 25Kb), do not take too long to download.

The main page itself contains numerous links, directing viewers to the various resources available on the site. Unfortunately, little planning seems to have gone into this collection, as the list of navigation link scrolls down for four or five screens, clustered together in a seemingly random basis.

Cybertown's main attraction is that it offers something for everyone - ranging from chat areas to educational resources and links, online classifieds, art galleries and more.

The only major negatives of the site are its use of predominantly black backgrounds and its poor page structure.

Whilst the dark backgrounds enhance the "space age" appearance of the graphics, it can cause legibility problems (especially for those with poor eyesight).

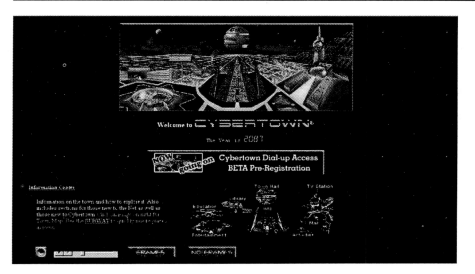

Cybertown is the kind of Web site you either love or hate on sight.

The overall navigation of the site is quite easy, as most of it occurs via a clickable map of the site. However, when visitors get to the individual areas, they are often forced to scroll through screen after screen of information to find what is on offer. The site would benefit from better planning through the use of categories and a more expansive hierarchy of pages.

GeoCities (www.geocities.com)

GeoCities has a fast-loading home page that is both crisp and compact. The main banner and navigation icons at the top of the page (the GeoCities logo etc.) are all quite small (some as small as 2K, nothing larger than 10Kb) — very compact indeed. Also, many of the graphics are re-used, which speeds up the display of individual Web pages.

Although it is longer than a single screen, most of the information and resources on offer are displayed at the top of the home page, with the result that most visitors do not have to scroll to access the various areas of the site.

Thanks to the effective use of typefaces and capital lettering, the directory listing of resources is quite legible, even though it uses a smaller-than-average font size. This in turn provides for conservative screen use, allowing more information to be displayed within a single screen.

Much of the content within the site itself is provided by individuals — GeoCities offers free Web hosting to anyone, and provides a search engine for Web sites within GeoCities so that visitors can find sites of interest. Once you get within the main GeoCities Web site and onto individual pages, you will encounter a wide variety of different designs — some professional, some amateurish, others in between.

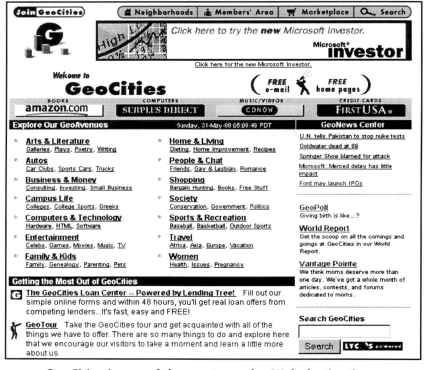

GeoCities is one of the most popular Web destinations.

SpellBound
(www.icontech.com/spellbound)

Spellbound is a Web site operated by a monster-truck hobbyist. It has a nice clean layout and uses "negative" (white) space quite well. While the typeface and font size makes the text easy to read, the use of all bold is a little unnerving. Bold type should as a general rule be reserved for headings or specific words that you want to emphasise.

The type itself goes right across the page, wrapping occasionally around the images, which can make it difficult to read, especially for new users who are used to newsprint-style margins.

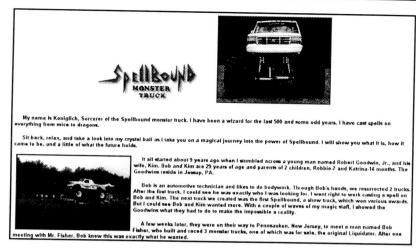

Unfortunately, the big truck equates to big images.

The biggest negative is image size. The site contains a number of colour photos. However, most have been saved in GIF format. As a result they are all quite large — the main image at the top of the page is 82Kb and the rest average around 40Kb. If the site's owner had saved the images as JPEGs, with extra compression or lower resolution, the photos could have been considerably smaller.

Layout is pretty simple, as befits a single-page Web site, and there aren't any other graphics to distract readers from the purpose of the Web site — the owner's pride and joy, his monster truck.

Although the site is mainly used to boast about the truck, it also appears to tout for business, although this aspect of the site is not highlighted very well. It also lacks any form of user interaction — no online feedback forms or email links, simply a telephone number!

Janet's Rocky Mountain Home Page
www.cowgirls.com/dream/jan/home.htm

Although the graphics are a fairly small (17Kb for the main graphic) it takes a while to load as the computer that hosts the Web site itself is a little slow (or, at least it was when we reviewed the site). However, it is an interesting site, with appealing illustrations and plenty of useful links to other western-theme Web sites. The colours used on the site are nice and earthy, giving visitors a feel of the countryside.

The site achieves what it sets out to do, which is to be a personal information and hobbyist site, providing a good resource for others with similar interests.

Janet's Rocky Mountain Home Page

The shortcomings are few: the heading lacks a bit of imagination, but this is perhaps the result of unfamiliarity with HTML. Also, the site lacks an introduction or some other summary of what it contains. Whilst the clickable navigation image on the home page is cute, it is not exactly informative.

A fairly appealing Web site.

Create Your Own Website
(www.net-works.co.uk/n8422.htm)

What can we say - a perfect site? Probably not. The page for this book is based around a two column table. In common with the rest of the site you will find links in a narrow column on the left providing easy navigation without having to scroll down the screen. The title is clear and in a red colour on white background for impact. The book cover graphic is small and loads in under a second. A neat link on the price a field follows you to see the price in any country around the world.

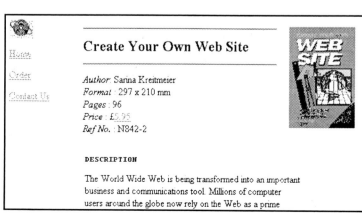

Create Your Own Web Site

Author: Sarina Kreitmeier
Format : 297 x 210 mm
Pages : 96
Price : £5.95
Ref No. : N842-2

DESCRIPTION

The World Wide Web is being transformed into an important business and communications tool. Millions of computer users around the globe now rely on the Web as a prime

If you have any comments on our site - good or bad - please let us know at:

sales@net-works.co.uk

Find What You Want on the Internet

The sheer size of the Internet's information resources is its biggest challenge. There is no central repository of all this information, nor it is catalogued or sorted in ordered fashion.

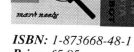
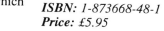

Find What You Want on The Internet is designed to teach Internet users - from novices to veterans - how to locate information quickly and easily.

The book uses jargon-free language, combined with many illustrations, to answer such questions as:

❑ Which search techniques and Search Engines work best for your specific needs?

❑ What is the real difference between true 'search' sites and on-line directories, and how do you decide which one to use?

ISBN: 1-873668-48-1
Price: £5.95

❑ How do the world's most powerful Search Engines really work?

❑ Are there any 'special tricks' that will help you find what you want, faster?

There is also a bonus chapter covering Intelligent Agents — special high-tech personal search programs that can be installed on your computer to search the Internet on your behalf, automatically.

Create Your Own Electronic Office

Home-based business... Cottage industry... Small Office/Home Office (SOHO)... whatever term you use, operating from home, means you escape the stresses, pressures and overheads of a busy town centre office. What-is-more, the time saved by not having to commute will allow you to work more efficiently and spend quality time enjoying yourself.

If this sounds like the kind of independence that you have dreamed of, then this book is for you. With its help, you will:

ISBN: 1-873668-44-9
Price: £5.95

● Decide whether working from home is for you;

● Equip your office with the right technology to make it efficient from day one:

● Plan your new business and working environment

Included are chapters on getting yourself motivated for working by yourself for yourself, how to maintain a healthy separation between your work and private life, and how to present yourself and your new business in a professional manner.

Complete Beginner's Guide to Word for Windows

Price: £5.95

Using Microsoft Word is a hit and miss process for a lot of people, and the end results are usually far from satisfying. What-is-more, many of the alternative books available are difficult to understand, and do not focus on the task of getting the job done, leaving you free to write creatively.

The Complete Beginner's Guide to Word for Windows is different. It has been designed and researched by the people who know best - the trainers who teach Word for a living. They understand both beginners and advanced students, and know how to meet their needs.

With clear, step-by-step instructions, and plenty of easy to understand examples, this book guides you to success the easy way. It leaves you free to concentrate on your document instead of getting the program to run properly!

Complete Beginner's Guide to Windows 98

Price: £5.95

An easy-to-read guide to Windows 98 with simple instructions and hundreds of useful illustrations. It leads you through everything from installing Windows 98 to exploring the many exciting features on offer such as the dynamic Active Desktop and revamped Explorer.

Also find out how to access the Internet using the Windows 98 Web browser, email program, newsgroup reader, Web page editor and even a Web publishing wizard. Then learn how to use the amazing "Internet Telephone" that lets you talk over the Net instead of making expensive STD or international calls. That's not all!

The Complete Beginner's Guide to Windows 98 uses plain English to explain all Windows 98 has to offer; making it perfect for novices and experienced computer users alike: Master the new and easy-to-use Address Book... Handle multimedia, both live on the Internet and from CD-ROM and DVD. You can even turn your PC into a TV set!... Share your windows PC by creating "user profiles" which allow several different users to customise and access the desktop... Recover valuable disk space with FAT32... Discover new improved utilities to keep your PC running smoothly: Disk Defragmenter, Disk Cleanup, Maintenance Wizard, Backup, and ScanDisk... Keep Windows up-to-date using the Internet.

The Complete Beginner's Guide to The Internet

What exactly is The Internet? Where did it come from and where is it going? And, more importantly, how can everybody take their place in this new community?

The Complete Beginner's Guide to The Internet answers all of those questions and more. On top of being an indispensable guide to the basics of Cyberspace,

☐   It is the lowest priced introduction on the market by a long way at a surfer-friendly £4.95. Who wants to spend £30+ on an alternative to find out The Internet is not for them?

☐   It comes in an easy-to-read format. Alternatives, with their 300+ pages, are intimidating even to those who are familiar with The Net, let alone complete beginners!

Price: £4.95

The Complete Beginner's Guide to The Internet tells you:

●   What types of resources are available for private, educational and business use,

●   What software and hardware you need to access them,

●   How to communicate with others, and

●   The rules of the Superhighway, or 'netiquette'.

Book Order Form

Please complete the form USING BLOCK CAPITALS and return to
TTL, PO Box 200, Harrogate HG1 2YR or fax to **01423-526035**

	Book	Qty	Price
☐ I enclose a cheque/postal order for £_____ made payable to '**TTL**'			
☐ Please debit my Visa/ Amex/Mastercard No:			

Postage: Over £8 free, otherwise please add 50p per item within UK. £1.50 elsewhere. **Total:**

Expiry date: ☐☐☐☐

Title: _____ Initials: _____

Signature:

Name: _____

Address: _____

Date:

Please allow 14-21 days delivery.

_____ Postcode: _____

We hope to make you further exciting offers in the future. If you do not wish to receive these, please write to us at the above address.

Daytime Telephone: _____

cyoweb